MEETINGS FOR SCHOOL-BASED DECISION MAKING

Meetings for School-Based Decision Making

KEEN J. BABBAGE, Ed.D.

TECHNOMIC
PUBLISHING CO., INC.

LANCASTER · BASEL

Meetings for School-Based Decision Making
aTECHNOMIC publication

Published in the Western Hemisphere by
Technomic Publishing Company, Inc.
851 New Holland Avenue, Box 3535
Lancaster, Pennsylvania 17604 U.S.A.

Distributed in the Rest of the World by
Technomic Publishing AG
Missionsstrasse 44
CH-4055 Basel, Switzerland

Printed in the United States of America
10 9 8 7 6 5 4 3 2 1

Main entry under title:
   Meetings for School-Based Decision Making

A Technomic Publishing Company book
Bibliography: p.
Includes index p. 107

Library of Congress Catalog Card No. 96-60908
ISBN No. 1-56676-450-5

CONTENTS

In October 1988, my brother, Bob, commented to me, "Keen, now that you are back in Lexington, you ought to go get a doctorate at UK." His tone was as casual as if he had said, "You ought to go get a pizza."

Four and a half years after following Bob's advice, I had completed my doctorate in educational administration from the University of Kentucky. It would have been much easier, but less rewarding, to have gotten a pizza.

The timing was perfect. In 1989, Kentucky was preparing for the 1990 session of the legislature in which the Kentucky Education Reform Act would be passed. Some of my professors were involved in helping create that new law. I shall forever be appreciative of my doctoral committee: Dr. Ron Threadgill, Dr. Charles Faber, Dr. Gary Anglin, Dr. Phil Roeder, Dr. Betty Steffy, Dr. Jane Lindle, and Dr. Eddy Van Meter.

My dissertation dealt with the public policy aspect of implementing school-based decision making (SBDM). Dr. Van Meter's start-to-finish guidance was essential. The many people in several Kentucky communities who allowed me to interview them were gracious and helpful. Thank you.

Soon after completing the doctorate, I became associate principal of Bryan Station Middle School in Lexington, Kentucky. I serve as a member of the school council.

There is one more personal acknowledgment—my older nephew, Robert. During the difficult months when I worked constantly on the dissertation and rarely saw my family, Robert, then age 5, left this message on my phone machine. "Uncle Keen, I hope you have a good dissertation."

I think I did, but with the dissertation and this book completed, it's time to go get a pizza with Bob and Robert.

It should be noted that the research done for this book draws upon two major sources: (1) my experiences as a doctoral student at the University of Kentucky and (2) my experiences from 1976–1995 as an employee of three large corporations and four schools, two public schools and two private schools. Throughout those two decades and seven jobs, I have attended countless meetings. The productive meetings provided some guidance. The unproductive meetings, in lacking what productive meetings have, confirmed what is needed for meetings that cause organizational improvement via making decisions and implementing decisions.

Decisions are made every day at every school. Many other decisions that impact schools are made elsewhere. These other decisions include those made by School Boards, state legislatures, governors, the United States Congress, a local city or county government, families, businesses, and community members.

The recent trend in school management and decision making parallels the trend in corporate management to push decision making authority to the level which best knows the issue at hand. In education, the people who best know a school are the people who work at that school, plus the families, students included, and the community members who are served by that school.

American education is approaching the day when no two schools will be exactly alike. The reason for this emerging variation is that each school will make decisions which are uniquely suited for the people and the circumstances of that school.

To base decisions about each unique school on the judgment of people associated with that school is a bold venture into managerial democracy.

Throughout the history of American education, decisions have been made daily "of, by and for the people" of each school. The principal may have made most decisions, but the principal did not decide how to cook lunch in the cafeteria, how many questions to ask on a test or what grade a student got in a class.

The process for making substantial, far-reaching policy decisions within a school is, in some schools, now done through the process of "school-based decision making" (SBDM). This is a formal process which uses elected or appointed members of a school council. The school council acts as the school's governing body.

Without the formal process of principals, teachers, parents, guardians, staff members, students and/or community members forming a school council to implement meetings for SBDM, a school can still base decisions for that school on what is needed uniquely for that school.

How will these decisions get made? Meetings. First grade teachers may meet to review how reading will be taught. Middle school science teachers may meet to review the curriculum for each grade. High school faculty and staff may meet to revise the school discipline policies.

The Parent Teacher Association may meet to host a discussion of the proposed school calendar for next year. The principal may meet with the school cafeteria staff to revise the lunch schedule or the breakfast clean-up process.

> The purpose of these multi-people meetings is to make decisions that improve the school and to assign responsibility to people who will carry out the decisions.

Schools are places where many decisions are made daily. Some of these decisions require the involvement of several people or of many people. These multi-people decisions often will require meetings. The purpose of these meetings is not to gather, sit, talk and schedule another meeting. The purpose of these multi-people meetings is to make decisions that improve the school and to assign responsibility to people who will carry out the decisions.

This book is about meetings that improve schools. All schools have meetings. Some of those meetings are productive, efficient and result in an improved school. Some of those meetings are painful wastes of time, which actually harm the school.

The ideas in this book can apply to any meeting at any school. However, the book is organized with school-based decision making meetings which use an official school council as the point of reference for how to plan for, manage and follow up meetings which improve schools. SBDM is this book's case study in creating better meetings.

For schools that have begun the formal process of school-based decision making, the terminology in this book will apply directly.

For schools that have not begun a formal SBDM process, please make the necessary mental editing of this book so the ideas presented here can apply to the types of meetings at any school.

Because school-based decision making is increasing in use throughout the United States, some specific SBDM information is included here. Because Kentucky had over 1,000 of its 1,400 public schools using SBDM in the 1995–1996 school year, much material in this book dealing specifically about school-based decision making is from Kentucky.

School-based decision making is the process by which each school makes decisions "of the people, by the people and for the people" at that school. Lincoln's ideal of democracy can come alive in school-based decision making.

The challenge is not to agree again that everyone associated with a school deserves to be involved in creating the future of the school. That agreement has already been reached. The challenge is to create the system which implements and operationalizes the democratic, decentralized, participatory management which school-based decision making can be.

To implement school-based decision making a school council can be used. This council can include one or more representatives of some or all of the following groups: administrators, teachers, parents or guardians, staff members, students and community members.

For a school council to be productive, it must have effective meetings that cause the school to improve. That is one goal.

For a school to be productive, it must have effective meetings which cause the school to improve. That is another goal. The ideas that follow can help educators, parents, guardians, students and citizens improve education via meetings that improve schools.

Decentralized Management—School Boards, Schools, and Meetings

Aristotle was wise when he concluded, "The diner, not the chef, is the best judge of a feast." Applied to management practices, Aristotle's thought requires that company executives listen to assembly line workers and actually defer some decisions to those workers. In school management, the parallel is for state governments and school boards to defer some decisions to the teachers, principals, parents and citizens associated with each school. Chapter 1 explores the concept of democratic, decentralized, participatory management in education.

"At our company we've been using labor-management teams for years. It started when a huge corporation acquired our company. They imposed a decentralized management system. We really listen to each other. We still have a boss and she has a boss, but everyone can be involved in the discussions. The workers don't try to run the place, but the managers know that worker input is helpful. Why don't schools do that?"

The school board members had asked for any comments from the public. The expected topics were a high school football team's coach and his three years of losing records, some excuses and blame for low test scores, plus the typical complaint about taxes being too high. The school board did not expect to hear a question about how schools make decisions.

The superintendent responded. "There are several places in the nation where what you suggested for us has been tried. It's called school-based management or school-based decision making. The school reforms in Chicago and Kentucky used this method. Sometimes a state or a school district has imposed this on schools to increase accountability and to tell each school that now there were no more excuses—you have power, so get results. Don't blame the bureaucracy or central office or the state. Why do you recommend it for us?"

"Well, I've seen it work at our company. For years the people on the assembly line knew what could be done better, but nobody asked us. We just kept making average products, getting paid and going home. The new president of our company changed that. His office door is open. He works the assembly line one shift per month. He organized a system of regular meetings so workers and bosses listen to each other. Our company is doing much better."

The television cameras were turned back on now. Reporters who thought the meeting was over could sense a story emerging. The newspaper reporter had almost left, but walked from the back of the room toward the front to hear this discussion.

One board member spoke up, "This makes sense. Companies all over the world have shown that sharing the decision making process with more employees is effective. Customers are also listened to. Can we set up a group to study this and report to us at our next meeting? I move that we do that."

The motion was approved and in two weeks the school board heard an initial report. The superintendent had assembled administrators, teachers, parents, and citizens. The gentleman who offered the idea was involved in the group. He presented the findings to the school board.

"Thank you. I am Andrew Procter. Since the last school board meeting there have been several of us who met to research and discuss different ways for schools to make decisions. Our goal is to find a way or to create a way for schools to involve everyone who is affected by schools to have the opportunity to be a participant in the major decisions that schools make. We have more work to do, but you asked for a report by tonight and we met your deadline. You each have a copy of our report and we've provided copies to everyone here tonight. I'd like to summarize our key conclusions and recommendations, please.

"First, our research and our discussions began with the idea of school-based management. This process means that a school board makes all major decisions for the school district, but that each school is allowed to or is encouraged to manage the implementation of those decisions in the way that works best for that school.

"School-based decision making is a more decentralized method of school-based management. School-based decision making says that the school is the place where decisions are made and managed. These decisions are within the broad direction of school board policies. We prefer the school-based decision making model and our report is premised on that.

"Second, there are enough good examples of schools which have successfully implemented school-based decision making to convince us that this idea is not a passing fad and to show us how to get started quickly.

"Third, the school board should have a policy about how school-based decision making will be implemented, but the policy should be flexible enough for each school to create its own by-laws and procedures according to what will work best there.

"Fourth, school-based decision making is not the cure for every problem in education. School-based decision making is a process which involves more people in the governance of a school and which has the potential to build new energy for improving schools, new ideas for improving schools and new commitment to improving schools.

"Fifth, school-based decision making requires much time and effort from many people. These people must know that their work will be worthwhile. When the school-based decision making council at a school meets, the meeting cannot have one person in control with everyone else silently going along. The meetings of a council must be based upon genuine democratic rights of free speech, free assembly and freedom to petition the government.

"Last, we propose that the school board authorize our group to write your policy on school-based decision making. With your agreement, we will present a proposed policy in two months."

The school board chair thanked Mr. Procter and the group. After substantial discussion, the board approved Mr. Procter's request; however, one change was made. In the spirit of democracy and of decentralized management, Mr. Procter's policy writing group was expanded to include more parents, guardians, teachers, students, principals, and community members. The participatory spirit and process of school-based decision making would begin now with the policy making process. It just makes sense for people who will implement the policy to be involved in creating the policy.

POLICY PROPOSALS

The school board received the school-based decision making policy proposal one week before the meeting when that policy would be initially presented. This gave all school board members adequate time to read the policy before the public meeting. The executive summary of the policy included interpretation and key points as provided by the school district's attorney and Mr. Procter.

Proposed Policy on School-Based Decision Making—Executive Summary

(1) School-based decision making could be seen as education's version of quality circles in a corporation, 800 numbers for consumers to report problems with a product and face-to-face interactive media sessions between politicians and voters.

(2) The proposed policy creates two major questions for the school board: (A) If each school carries out school-based decision making by establishing a school council to govern its school, what responsibility and authority will the school board still have? (B) When a school board and a school's council disagree over which group has the final authority, can these disputes be resolved without a court case?

(3) The membership of each school's council as proposed in the policy is nine people—the principal, three teachers, three parents or guardians, one community member from the school's attendance area, and one classified employee of the school. One concern is whether each school can find willing participants. A second concern is that since voluntary participation in other recent school improvement plans has been low, what will make participation in this any different?

(4) The policy gives each school's council authority over curriculum, extra-curricular activities and hiring of all professional employees. This creates the possibility that no two schools in the school district would have the same curriculum, which will create problems when students transfer from one school to another. The school that sets the lowest requirements for participation in extra-curricular activities, including sports, may have an unfair advantage and may mislead its students. Council members could be subject to legal challenges if people who are not properly trained in interviewing and in hiring ask an inappropriate question of a job applicant.

(5) The policy requires that each school council meet twice per month.

This creates a time burden on people who are already stretched to their limit.

(6) The policy calls for school-based decision making to be implemented by each school in this district within one year. If schools already have a version of a school council in place, why make them change? If school-based decision making is mandated, will it work as well as when it is accepted voluntarily?

(7) This proposed policy asks for each school to be allocated its portion of district money for textbooks and school supplies. This will create bookkeeping confusion and may result in the need for additional bookkeepers who can help each school manage its financial records.

(8) The policy empowers the school council to select its chairman. There could be some complications and some legal problems if the principal is not the chairman.

Overall recommendation: Move steadily on this. Gather more input from schools that have used SBDM. Consider testing SBDM next year in one or two schools. Consider testing simultaneously at one or two other schools the option of school-based management. The management option gives the school board the authority to make decisions that are then implemented or managed by a council or committee at each school. School-based decision making gives each school the authority to make decisions and to implement decisions.

SCHOOL BOARD DECISION

School-Based Decision Making with a Council

After two school board meetings at which the school-based decision making policy was proposed, read, and discussed, the school board decided to receive applications from schools that would like to try having a school council. One elementary and one secondary school would be selected to test school-based decision making, plus, two schools would test school-based management.

The final policy would be approved after those test schools were chosen so they could help write the policy. After testing for one year, the school board would determine the best way to proceed.

Requirements

Two requirements were added by the school board. First, each teacher in the test schools will serve on a committee of the school council. The school board members concluded that school-based decision making would work only if all teachers were involved. Second, twelve hours of training would be required for any school council member prior to serving on a council. The school board realized that most teachers, parents, guardians, classified employees, community members, and students have not been trained in methods of leadership and management for a school.

Some people saw these requirements from the school board as unnecessary restrictions imposed by the board members who wanted to show that they were still in control even with a new system of decentralization. Other people saw these requirements as wise safeguards which the board required in order to help school-based decision making succeed. The debate over the motive of the school board in making these two requirements was a signal that, similar to the national government and fifty states, there would be a continuous battle between a school board and the district's school councils over jurisdiction, authority, and control.

The school board made one other decision. The school board members agreed that responsibility for the quality of education should rest with the employees of each school. School-based decision making would enable the two test schools to function in a near autonomous way, which resembled the southern states under the constitution of the Confederate States of America. School-based management would have some autonomy, but less than SBDM.

School-Based Decision Making without a Council

The school board selected two other schools to test a school-based management system without using a school council. This system called for an administrator from the two selected schools to attend each school board meeting and offer the perspective of front line practitioners. The school board members hoped that this would enable them to make decisions which would be more sensitive to school realities. With one elementary school principal and one secondary school principal directly involved with the school board, the process of (1) decisions made by the school board and (2) those decisions implemented by each school may be improved. This provided a different method of participatory school-based management without going to the extent of school-based decision making.

The school board acknowledged that no two schools are identical; therefore, some variance must be allowed as each school serves its students. The question becomes: how much uniformity among schools in a school district is necessary versus how much decentralized variation can be allowed between schools? School-based management acknowledges the need for each school to manage its affairs and to implement decisions from above in its way. School-based decision making is an extended form of school-based management. SBDM permits both the decision making and the implementation of the decision to occur at the school level.

MANAGERIAL DEMOCRACY

Who gets credit for the idea of managerial democracy such as school-based decision making? We might give credit to Aristotle whose thought cited earlier—"The diner, not the chef, is the best judge of a feast"—is true to participatory management and to democratic decision making.

We could share some credit with Abraham Lincoln because SBDM is "government of the people, by the people and for the people."

If we paraphrase John Kennedy we could credit him. "Ask not what your school can do for you, ask what you can do for your school. Ask not what the school board will do for you, but what together we can do for the education of our students."

The bold methods of changing the structure and the processes in American corporations during the 1980s and 1990s deserve some credit for showing any organization that the old hierarchy need not endure forever. The examples from the Peters and Waterman book *In Search of Excellence* or from Waterman in *The Renewal Factor* include corporate versions of school-based decision making.

From Aristotle's concepts of democracy through corporate quality circles, why has there been a persistent voice calling for democratic, decentralized, participatory management? Dr. Earl Reum, the driving force behind programs which taught millions of students about leadership in recent decades, gives this clear answer: "People support what they help create."

School-based decision making creates a process that enables people to be involved in creating the future of their school. The hope is that people will help support that school because they are helping create what that school will be.

School-based decision making is one way to formally implement managerial democracy and is one process for school improvement. SBDM is not the only way to bring more participation to the decision making procedures at a school and SBDM is not the only process for school improvement.

Some of the rationale for, philosophy of, and procedures for school-based decision making could be useful at a school that decided not to formally institutionalize the SBDM process. The fundamental question here is not simply "to have SBDM or not to have SBDM." The fundamental question here is, "Since any process of improving schools will involve meetings, how can we create meetings that improve schools?"

Most emerging methods of decision making and decision implementing are more democratic and more participatory than earlier processes. Most of these emerging methods include more communication and more meetings—whether it is face to face between two people or whether it is a formal, structured, scheduled, "sit down" gathering of a larger group.

Be careful—democracy is inefficient and chaotic. Giving everyone the opportunity to participate in decisions can create as many possibilities for disagreement as it does for consensus, but the possibility will exist that people can work together to create a common purpose for a school and that everyone involved can commit themselves to achieving that common purpose for the school. Democracy is an exhausting adventure, but it can produce superior results.

Be bold: school-based decision making can enable real leaders to be better leaders. The purpose of leadership is to get the best results in the best way.

Leaders, real leaders, are equally concerned about how they obtain results as they are about actually obtaining the results.

The purpose of leadership is to get the best results in the best way.

Principals, superintendents, or school board members who see SBDM as a threat to their power or to their empire reveal their misunderstanding of leadership. The purpose of a school is to cause learning. Learning is not caused when power battles, turf wars or ego clashes make school officials act as if they are video game warriors.

The purpose of a school is to cause learning.

When an administrator works with teachers, students, parents, guardians, and the community the possibility for real leadership is enhanced. When the administrator excludes these people, he or she may amass power over a school and may have an impact on the school, but the dictatorial methods of fear, intimidation, and threats create a cruel atmosphere where real leading and healthy learning are diminished.

Be resourceful: the trail blazing in SBDM has been done. Borrow from the experiences that Australian and Canadian schools have had with decentralized management. Read the results of Chicago's use of school-based decision making. Study the learning from Kentucky where schools began SBDM in 1990 as part of the Kentucky Education Reform Act (KERA) and where almost all public schools will have school-based decision making by 1996–1997. As of 1996, over 1,000 of Kentucky's 1,400 public schools had begun using SBDM.

Most school teachers and administrators dream of having more involvement in their school by parents and guardians. Many teachers dream of administrators who will listen to them. Many administrators dream of people who will help them carry the load. Parents and community members often wonder, "What are those educators up to now?" Newspapers write editorials encouraging everyone to participate more in schools.

School-based decision making is one process that can provide a method of involving these groups of people in such a way that involvement is worthwhile. SBDM can deal with the essential aspects of a school such as curriculum, discipline, new employee selection, professional development of teachers, how students are graded and how time during the school day is allocated.

Despite cellular phones, electronic mail, laptop computers and video everything, most school activity is still face-to-face. There is a reason for that—teaching and learning are intimate human adventures. Much of education still requires that people are together. School-based decision making has this requirement because democracy, especially in its infancy, needs the human interaction which comes only through proximity. SBDM will require meetings so people can work together in person. For SBDM to work the meetings must work. Attention now turns to the purposes for and the mechanics of these meetings.

CHAPTER 2

Why Use Meetings to Make Decisions and to Implement Decisions?

Educators are too busy. Parents and citizens are too busy. There is no time for another meeting.

One reason that everyone is so busy may be that everyone is trying to do everything alone. Teaming up, trading ideas, dividing responsibilities, and building common bonds of commitment to shared goals could bring more results with new efficiency. The method for this group venture is meetings.

This chapter acknowledges the difficulties that meetings can encounter but confirms that meetings can bring energy, efficiency, and direction to decentralized management of schools.

Imagine that each student attended his or her own school. It would be very easy to take attendance, to supervise the cafeteria, to individualize instruction and to make schedule changes. What would be so simple for a school of one student becomes very complex with schools of hundreds or thousands of students.

Imagine driving through a town as the only driver on any street. There is no traffic. Every light is green. It would be very easy to travel throughout the town with no traffic, no red lights and no other vehicles. What would be so simple for one driver in one car becomes very complex with hundreds of streets and thousands of cars.

Now, imagine two young adults who are each single. Life is not very complicated or complex for this twenty-four-year-old man and for this twenty-five-year-old woman. They each work, pay bills, have an apartment and have fun with friends. These two people meet at a party and soon begin dating. Their schedules have to give and take a little so they can be together. They have to agree on which restaurant or which movie. These are not difficult decisions, but they are decisions made jointly by two people and that means some interaction had to occur. This is unlike the old days, before they started dating, when each person just followed personal preferences.

If these two young people decide to get married, they will enter into a wonderful, complex, adventurous, and complicated relationship. Marriage could be a process through which they share love, joy, commitment and goals. Marriage will include some disagreements, tragedy, and pain. To make the marriage work, the couple will need to have frequent meetings of mind, heart, and soul. The couple will also need to be together to communicate, to trade ideas and to make decisions. Life will be more complicated with the duties of a marriage, but it can become more fulfilling.

If each human being lives in isolation on individual islands, there is no need for meetings and there is no need for school-based decision making. The reality is that most people will live most of their lives as active and as interactive members of a family, neighborhood, school, church, company, or other employer, club, organization, audience, and/or traffic. Life is mostly interactive. One way to interact is in a meeting.

PICTURING THE TYPICAL MEETING

When the word *meeting* is heard, what picture comes to mind? A large group of bored people who are struggling to stay awake as they sneak another look at their watch and think, "Will this ever end?" Heads nodding in sleepy agreement as one more confusing chart is shown and one more unclear slide is projected to show why what one person has already decided is what we should all endorse? Notebooks, handouts, coffee cups, legal pads, flip charts plus an agenda that gets disregarded after the first five minutes.

Does the word *meeting* suggest (1) the efficient communication of important information; (2) an intellectual democracy where facts, ideas and opinions can collide until truth emerges; and/or (3) a gathering that concludes with specific decisions made and specific assignments of duties for implementing those decisions with definite deadlines?

Do the words "We need to set up a meeting about that" inspire people to prepare for the meeting and participate in it or to dread it? Who has time for one more meeting? At a time when schools are asked to feed, counsel, cure, educate, train, exercise, and protect each student, how can we schedule one more meeting?

Meetings are going to be held in schools, about schools, and for schools. The question is not, "How can we reduce the number of meetings?" Although that may be a worthy goal and a feasible objective. The question is "How can we increase the efficiency of and the productivity of meetings?"

Schools do not need to schedule meetings just because "the budget committee has not met for several months" or because "the committee meets every third Wednesday whether we need to or not." Schools need to schedule purposeful, necessary meetings that are prepared for, well managed, and followed-up.

ONE MORE MEETING?

School-based decision making is not creating "one more meeting." School-based decision making may create *the* meeting. When the SBDM meeting is held properly, some other meetings may become unnecessary. SBDM will require preparation, time, and follow-up, but if this management and governance method actually solves problems, then other hours spent chasing elusive solutions could be redirected to implementing decisions made by the school council, SBDM council, or other term given to the group that SBDM authorized or that a school is using to coordinate overall management and/or school improvement.

Communication

How do people in schools communicate? Most communication occurs in the informality of two or more people just seeing each other for a few moments. As the principal completes hall duty a teacher may start a quick conversation to update the principal about phone calls from a parent of a student who was in trouble recently. Teachers may discuss school topics at lunch. The copy machine waiting line may be a time and place for conversations.

Any of these informal, unplanned discussions are part of the minute-to-minute, day-to-day life of any work place. These conversations may include the sharing of important information, may build friendships, may identify problems, may lead to nothing, may serve ulterior motives or may be pure gossip. These conversations rarely have the substance of authority or the appearance of official, formal action. For legitimate decision making that will impact much or all of the school, a more structured and formal process will be needed.

Communication Methods

What other communication methods are common in schools? Public address (PA) systems are commonly used and are commonly cursed. The PA has the chilling impact of an ambulance's siren. The PA may inform some people some of the time about some events at school; however, PA announcements are often followed by a chorus from the audience of "What did they say?" PA systems are used to speak at people rather than to talk with people. The PA will not do much good for the interactive communication which is necessary for school-based decision making.

> Memos serve a purpose in a total plan of effective communication, but no school ever became great due to superior memos.

Can memos help? The answer is yes, but memos alone are not enough. Memos provide information and may make requests for information. Memos permit all people who need the information to read, reread, think and react as their schedule allows. In the SBDM process, memos can help people prepare for a meeting by providing necessary background information. Memos can help complete the communication circuit after a meeting by providing a record of decisions made and topics discussed. Memos serve a purpose in a total plan of effective communication, but no school ever became great due to superior memos.

Can e-mail or other forms of instant, computer correspondence help? Does a fax machine help? Would cordless phones or an interactive intercom system throughout the building help? These methods are swift and are convenient, but they exclude face-to-face interaction. If a school has a computer in each classroom, electronic mail can be a more humane version of the PA system and it may be the emerging preference for communicating with colleagues without having to get everyone's schedule to mesh, but SBDM is up-close and personal. High tech communication methods are tools of school-based decision making, but they are not the ultimate method.

Process and Goals

In SBDM the process is as important as the product. The method of making the decision is as important as the actual decisions.

SBDM is a process that can create consensus for and commitment to decisions that can improve a school. Sure, decisions can be made via memos or several rounds of e-mail, but in SBDM the process is as important as the product. The method of making the decision is as important as the actual decisions.

Decisions have always been made about schools. If all we needed was more decisions for schools there would be no need for SBDM. What is realized now is that a school needs to humanly, humanely, and democratically create solutions and plans which will cause improvement for that school. People and conditions vary from school to school; therefore, solutions and plans need to vary. A democratic, decentralized, participatory process using efficient, results-oriented meetings can help create the solutions and plans a school needs.

Even with varied solutions and plans uniquely suited for each school, the effective implementation of those ideas will be enhanced if consensus and commitment are built as the ideas are considered and approved. SBDM puts into operation a process through which commitment, consensus, solutions, and plans can emerge. For this process to be maximized, people need to be together in meetings. People are more likely to build bonds through proximity. People can be aware of each other through the exchange of post cards, letters, pictures, e-mail, faxes, and teleconferences. School improvement needs the participants to be more than aware of each other. People need to be on the same team, people need to be part of the consensus about what the purpose of their school is and people need to make mutual commitments to improving their school together. Those people who would improve a school need to meet.

The goal is not merely to have a meeting. The goal is to cause a school to improve by creating consensus for and commitment to decisions which will improve the school and to responsibility for implementing those decisions that will improve the school. There will be no points given to people whose only result after a year of SBDM is, "Well, we sure had a lot of meetings." Points will be given to schools that make and implement decisions (A) that are uniquely appropriate for the conditions at and for the people at that school and (B) that have consensus from and commitment from those people.

The goal is to cause a school to improve by creating consensus for and commitment to decisions that will improve the school and to responsibil ity for implementing those decisions that will improve the school.

TYPICAL MEETINGS

Think for a minute of meetings which people typically attend. Examples would include a faculty meeting, a PTA meeting, a church meeting, a little league preseason meeting, or a similar gathering. What was different about the meetings that were very successful? Were they started on time? Did they end on time? Did every question asked get an answer? Was the agenda shared in advance of the meeting? Was the agenda followed? Did the leader of the meeting emphasize results such as decisions, assignment of duties and agreement on deadlines? Were people comfortable? Could everyone hear all comments and discussion?

What was true about unsuccessful meetings? Were people late? Did the meeting go on and on with no intention of resolving matters? Was the seating arrangement one which left some people out? Were people unable to hear? Was the agenda ignored or was there no agenda at all? Did one person or a few people dominate all discussion and all decisions? Did it seem as if the meeting was just a way to appease people who could now be told, "You had your meeting—what else could you want?"

The reputation which school-based decision making earns at a school will significantly be affected by the quality of meetings which the SBDM school council has. Why do Americans have such a low opinion of the U.S. Congress? One reason is that the televised meetings seen on C-SPAN appear to be either fully unorganized or fully contrived, plus their discussions do not seem to be about topics or about information that relate to the lives of typical Americans. Congress seems to be having their meetings, in their way, for their reasons that only they understand.

There is not one perfect model for a meeting which every organization must follow. A corporation's Board of Directors, a city council's town meeting on a proposed zoning change, a session of a convention, a family reunion or a school council will have different purposes for their meetings and will need to establish the method which most effectively serves their purposes. Still, some aspects of successful meetings can be shared by all of those groups, while leaving room for uniqueness.

The point has been made already that an SBDM meeting cannot be "just another meeting." This caution tells educators that the SBDM school council cannot just be added to the list of existing meetings and seen as one more demand on already crowded schedules. Also, this caution tells educators that a productive and proper school council meeting is not identical to every other or any other school meeting. SBDM meetings are unique in importance, in content, and in format. The type of meeting a school has for SBDM needs to reflect the uniqueness of what school-based decision making is and of what that school needs SBDM to do. Still, there are universal qualities of good meetings, which will be itemized further in Chapters 4 and 5.

School councils will operationalize the ideas and the process of democratic, decentralized, participatory management. School council meetings will be the most visible and the most significant aspect of operationalizing and implementing democratic, decentralized, participatory management. The meetings are intended to create consensus for and commitment to decisions that will improve the school and to assignment of duties that will cause the decisions to be implemented.

JURISDICTION

Legal

School council meetings will be limited to the topics that are within the jurisdiction of the school council. School council meetings are to emphasize policies, procedures, and priorities for the school.

School council meetings are not the place for personal attacks or for personnel evaluations. School council meetings are not the place for a parent to complain about a discipline decision made about his or her child. A school council could discuss school discipline policies in general.

Kentucky's education reform law of 1990 assigned eight areas of authority to school councils. Decisions made by school councils in these eight areas are expected to be consistent with policies of the local school board; however, a school council may request a waiver from school board policy.

The exact wording from the Kentucky law is important. A summary is shown in Figure 2.1. Details are in Appendix A.

KENTUCKY EDUCATION REFORM ACT - 1990

Authority Given to School Councils

1. Determination of curriculum.

2. Assignment of all instructional and non-instructional staff time.

3. Assignment of students to classes and programs within the school.

4. Determination of the schedule of the school day and week, subject to the beginning and ending times of the school day and school calendar as established by the local board.

5. Determination of use of school space during the school day.

6. Planning and resolution of issues regarding instructional practices.

7. Selection and implementation of discipline and classroom management techniques.

8. Selection of extra curricular programs.

    Under these legal guidelines it would be perfectly acceptable for a school council at any public school in Kentucky to discuss the following topics:

    • Requiring all 8th graders to take Algebra

    • Use of computer software in an elementary school reading program

    • Block scheduling

    • A drug abuse education program

    • Increasing consequences for students who break school rules

    • Rewards for students who obey school rules

    • Having a computer lab or placing the computers in classrooms

    • The grade point average required for participation in sports or clubs

    • How to prepare students for annual tests

Figure 2.1. KERA: *School Council Authority Source: Kentucky Revised Statutes Chapter 160, section 14 (2) (I) (7-18).*

18

Limitations

Of course, many other topics could also be discussed. There is an equally important range of topics which a Kentucky school council should *not* discuss:

- one parent's complaint about one teacher's homework policy
- the cafeteria menu
- a discipline decision made about a particular student
- grades made by particular students
- the evaluation of teachers
- which students ride a school bus and which students will not be transported on a school bus
- rumors or gossip
- salaries of school employees
- the job description of a school counselor

There are other topics that a school council has no authority over and, therefore, should not discuss. The point is this: school councils must be given important areas of jurisdiction; however, some matters are still in the full authority of the school board or are among the administrative duties of a principal.

It would be unprofessional for a school council meeting to digress into an opinionated battle which places the supporters of a teacher against the opponents of that teacher. This could also result in a grievance or in a more serious legal action.

School council meetings will be more productive when the topics discussed and resolved are policies, not personalities or are ideas not accusations.

Is it illegal for the school council to discuss the process a school uses to dismiss students who walk, have a ride or use a school bus? No, but is this the best use of a school council's time? If a person has a real concern about this it could be discussed with the principal, it could be considered at a faculty meeting or evaluated by the PTA.

School councils and any other group meeting about a school must avoid the topics which are not in their jurisdiction. School councils and other committees, organizations, departments, or groups are wise to avoid topics that can be resolved in a more efficient way, perhaps by other people.

Meetings Are SBDM Made Visible

The most visible aspect of school-based decision making will be the meetings of the school council. To the extent that people perceive that these meetings are productive, purposeful and professional, school-based decision making will earn support. If school council meetings are perceived as petty, superficial, and aimless, school-based decision making will earn scorn.

The theories of democracy, participatory management, decentralization, accountability, or local control cannot be seen. These theories can be discussed, evaluated, and understood; however, it is the processes that implement any of these theories or ideals that can be seen. In school-based decision making, it is the school council meeting that can be seen, participated in, "touched" by people. School council meetings are the formal, public test that school-based decision making must clearly pass if this process of managing and of leading a school is to succeed and is to be perceived as having succeeded.

For school-based decision making to work at its best, a school council will need much involvement from many people. Ways to obtain that necessary involvement from teachers, staff, families, and the community are the next topic. First, a word about application. School-based decision making continues to serve as the case study for this book. SBDM school council meetings can be meetings that improve schools and, due to authority given exclusively to a school council, these meetings may surpass others in the exercise of power. This does not mean that other school meetings can decline in quality, efficiency, or productivity. The methods that make a good SBDM school council meeting will generally work for any other meeting of two or more people with some authority for and responsibility for improving a school.

Teachers, Staff, Parents, Students, Community—Getting Involvement from All Groups

> Suppose we had a democratic, decentralized, participatory manage-
> ment system and nobody got involved. The result would be no results.
> Every educator laments the limited involvement of parents, guardians and
> the community in school work. There are ways to seek, to earn and to gain
> new involvement as Chapter 3 will show.

Ask them. Ask them individually. Ask them individually and sincerely. Ask them often. Involvement from teachers, staff, parents, students and community members must be sought. SBDM creates a new
process into which increased involvement may be very productively applied; however, SBDM itself will do little to motivate involvement from
people who are not currently involved.

If people who are not involved in a school are asked their reasons to
avoid involvement, would anyone say, "It's because our school does not
have school-based decision making"? No, their reasons include, "I don't
have time," or "I hated school when I was a student," or "They won't listen to me."

These comments imply that, for some teachers, staff, parents, students, and community members, getting involved is not worth the time or
the effort. If involvement included attending efficient and productive
meetings, there could be a greater willingness to be involved.

The announcement that a school will now fully incorporate school-
based decision making probably will not bring a standing room only
crowd to the first informational meeting. The announcement does create
an opportunity to ask people to get involved. The announcement also

gives a new justification for the time and effort that involvement requires—the people who participate in SBDM can actually help create the future for the school. SBDM is not a punch and cookies reception. SBDM is a real exercise of authority, power and responsibility. For every person who ever really sought to impact a school, SBDM, or any similar school-based improvement method can be part of what they have desired. That opportunity to directly impact a school needs to be communicated clearly, directly, individually, and often.

INCREMENTAL IMPROVEMENT

Victory can be declared when there is an increase in the involvement from teachers, staff, parents, guardians, students, and community members. Schools do not need to attain 100% participation from all of those groups before claiming that involvement has improved. If the SBDM system of committees, a school council and open-to-the-public meetings brings an increase in involvement, an increase in interaction, an increase in the number of people who are participating in building consensus for

Group	Actions that can be taken to involve members of this group in SBDM or in other school improvement meetings
Teachers	1.
	2.
	3.
Staff	1.
	2.
	3.
Parents, Guardians	1.
	2.
	3.
Students	1.
	2.
	3.
Community	1
	2.
	3.

Figure 3.1. Increasing Involvement in SBDM.

decisions which will improve our school, and/or an increase in the number of people who accept part of the duty of implementing those decisions, a school is making progress.

Most aspects of life are incremental. Individuals and groups take small steps. Persistence in taking many small steps in the same direction will lead people toward and to their goal. Meetings that improve schools are no different.

OK, some work must now be done. Take a few minutes to think and then fill in Figure 3.1.

COMMUNICATION THAT REACHES OUT

What is the difference between reaching out to potential activists with a television commercial that tells people about SBDM and a phone call that tells a person about SBDM? Could both methods be helpful?

A sample TV commercial, produced and broadcast by a local television station as part of their responsibility to the community and as a response to requests from the local school district, follows:

"Schools have always taught about democracy. Now schools are practicing democracy. In a management method called school-based decision making, a school council is established with members elected by parents, teachers and the community. The principal and a student are also on the school council. This council has decision making authority over major aspects of the school including curriculum and the scheduling of the school day. So, now schools teach democracy by example. To get involved in a school council, call the principal of the school nearest you."

A sample phone call, from a teacher, staff member, parent, student, or community member to another person in one of those groups, follows:

Ellen: Hi, this is Ellen Moorley. My daughter and your son, Brian, go to Grant Middle School together. Could I talk to you for a few minutes, please, about our new school council?
Parent: OK, but I don't have much time.
Ellen: You are right. Everyone is busy. I'll just take a minute. Our school

is starting a new process called school-based decision making. It means that each school will get to make its own decisions based on what is needed. We'll have a school council with parents, teachers and the principal. The school council will have meetings which are open to the public and even if people are not elected to the council they can serve on a school council committee.

Parent: Yeah. Does it cost me anything?

Ellen: No, sir. There is no cost. I just wanted to tell you about the school council and to invite you to a meeting a week from Monday at 7:00 P.M. at school. We'll have more information available then. I'll send you a brochure to tell you more and to remind you about the meeting.

Parent: OK. I need to go.

Ellen: Thanks for your time. Bye.

Which communication method is best—the commercial, the phone call, or the brochure? That is the wrong question. Try this: would each communication method be helpful? Yes. OK, do them all. The person who got the phone call may see the television commercial in a few days and will also receive the brochure in the mail. That person may begin to think that these school council organizers really know what they are doing!

Whether a school is starting a school council or whether a school council has been functioning for several years, there is a continual need to make the effort to involve people in school-based decision making. Thorough, constant, individual communication is vital. Establish a phone network so one person calls ten other people per month to tell them about the school council. That does take time and work. Democracy does not spontaneously generate itself or automatically sustain itself.

It is also vital that the school council keeps its promise to listen to people. If teachers, staff, parents, and the community are going to be told that the school council has the authority to create the school's future, then the council has to be allowed to do that. Don't promise democracy and then ignore people who present ideas, questions, or disagreements. Democracy is not improving the school as only one person wants to improve it. The task is to improve the school, not to accumulate personal power.

When watching or hearing the national or international news, reactions to the stories could often be, "Yeah, that's awful, but what can I do about it?" People may have similar responses to stories on the local news or in the local newspaper.

Schools can be improved, one at a time, if many people in each school and in its community will implement solutions made of, by and for their school.

Education is different. Every problem at every school in the country cannot be fixed by getting one person to implement one solution which is imposed on all schools. Schools can be improved, one at a time, if many people in each school and in its community, will implement solutions made of, by, and for their school.

If school personnel will communicate to people that participation in school-based decision making is a productive response that they can make to concerns in their community, a significant renewal of local parent and citizen involvement in schools would be inspired. To do that we need to communicate often, sincerely and individually. That is a simple idea that needs no complexity or complication; rather, it just needs to be done.

TO DO LIST

It is sometimes helpful to have a system or a "to do" list. In the area of getting involvement from all groups, here's a system to use for every person who is determined to help SBDM succeed at their school:

(1) Talk to and listen to teachers.

(2) Talk to and listen to staff members.

(3) Talk to and listen to parents or guardians.

(4) Talk to and listen to students.

(5) Talk to and listen to community members.

(6) Send newsletters to all groups in points 1–5.

(7) Schedule school council meetings at a time which is convenient for all groups.

(8) Get information about the school council in the newspaper, on TV, on radio, in local businesses, in civic group newsletters, in church bulletins, in or on grocery store bags, everywhere.

(9) Be sure each family in the school is called monthly about school council work, topics, meetings.

(10) Repeat steps 1, 2, 3, 4, and 5.

(11) Provide transportation or car pools for people who can't get to a school council meeting or to a committee meeting.

(12) Act upon every idea, comment, or question offered to the school council. Act upon does not guarantee approval of the idea, or agreement with the comment or a "make everyone happy" answer to the question. Act upon does guarantee serious consideration, plus a response to the person who originated the idea, comment or question.

(13) When people offer a suggestion, put them on the committee that will create a recommendation.

(14) Say thank you to people who participate in the school council and in the committees. Show your appreciation in tangible ways if allowed by law and policy. We do not need fancy gifts—a birthday card or a school T-shirt may be plenty.

(15) Once again—repeat steps 1–5 and be sure that other people are implementing steps 1–5.

(16)

(17)

(18)

(19)

(20)

Steps 16–20 are for more ideas to be filled in and then to do!

A LESSON FROM KENTUCKY

Another lesson can be taken from Kentucky. In April 1990 the Kentucky Education Reform Act was passed by the legislature and was signed by the governor. It would become effective ninety days later, in July 1990.

KERA was a 1,000-page law, which completely changed every part of public schools in Kentucky on a rapid schedule of full implementation by 1996. All of the 176 school districts in Kentucky were required to have at least one school using school-based decision making in the 1991–1992 school year. To prepare for this, all school districts had to submit their policy on school-based decision making to the Kentucky Department of Education by January 1, 1991.

KERA requires that all public schools in Kentucky implement school-based decision making by 1996–1997 with limited exceptions. Some schools began in 1990–1991, soon after KERA went into effect. Two-thirds of Kentucky's public schools had implemented school-based decision making as of the start of the 1995–1996 school year.

Schools in Kentucky are moving to school-based decision making ahead of the 1996 requirement for many reasons, including favorable results from some of the first schools to use SBDM. There is at least one serious concern—participation in elections for parent/guardian members of school councils has been very low on the average. Also, participation on school council committees and attendance at school council meetings rarely exceeds the few people who are required to attend.

Why? One reason is that few Kentucky school districts used the time between April 1990 and January 1, 1991 to involve teachers, parents, guardians, students, principals and the community in the process of creating a policy about school-based decision making. Most districts relied very heavily on a model policy which was provided by the Kentucky School Boards Association. Twenty-two of the 176 school districts in Kentucky adopted that model policy verbatim.

It appears that most districts in Kentucky missed the unique opportunity in 1990 to teach educators, families and citizens about school-based decision making. Admittedly, some school district leaders knew too little about SBDM to teach people what it was, but some districts made the effort to hire consultants, to have professional development meetings or to create a SBDM policy task force. Great communication with and increased participation from constituents can occur with much effort and with a high priority being given to that effort.

Now that ways to encourage people to become involved in school-based decision making have been identified, a consideration of the methods that can create meetings that improve schools is the next topic. The combination of much involvement and productive meetings can be a significant part of improving a school. The next topic is the most practical aspect of school-based decision making and of most comprehensive efforts to improve school—the actual meetings that can improve schools.

How to Make Meetings Work Better

At the end of too many meetings the only item that has been passed is time. There were few decisions. There were no responsibilities accepted by people who would implement the decisions. There was talk. For people who seek aimless conversation, radio and television talk shows are available. For people who seek to improve schools, purposeful and productive meeting techniques are available.

Chapter 4 requires that the reader become a writer and an interactive participant. Chapter 4 also introduces the "Decision Agenda" which, combined with a precise statement of school purpose, can help create meetings that improve schools. This chapter includes a case study based on a committee meeting.

As has been done throughout this book, the term *school council* will continue to be used to refer to the duly chosen group that is authorized to exercise the power of SBDM at a school. States, school districts, or schools may use a different name, but in this book as in the Kentucky SBDM experience, school council is the terminology.

This chapter will assume that a school council includes an administrator, some teachers, and some parents or guardians. The administrator would almost always be the principal. The teachers who are members will be elected by the faculty. The parents or guardians will be elected by all parents and guardians.

There are valid variations on the membership of a school council. If the school has more than one administrator, provisions can be made to include more than the principal. The term *certified staff* could be used instead of *teachers* to insure involvement of counselors, librarians, and other professional staff members who are assigned primarily to the school. Classified employees who work primarily at a school — teacher aides, library aides, office workers, cafeteria workers, custodial staff—could also be represented. Having a student member may make sense, especially in secondary schools, although due to some legal concerns it may be better for the student to be a non-voting member. Local citizens who are not parents or guardians could provide valuable input.

School council meetings need to be open to the public. It is vital that SBDM be synonymous with access and with interaction. If a state or school district has laws or policies about open meetings, those are the standard. If such laws are not in use, the school council may adopt a policy about open meetings.

School-based decision making is more comprehensive than school-based management or site-based management. As Dr. Charles Faber from the University of Kentucky has explained, school-based decision making means that people at one school are making the decisions for that school and are implementing those decisions. School-based management or site-based management could be a process of people at one school managing the implementation of decisions made at another place—the school board, the central office, the state legislature, the state's department of education—by other people.

PREPARATION

> Without proper preparation the meeting will fall far short in efficiency and in productivity of what it could have been.

Preparation. The one word *preparation* is the best answer to the question, "What makes a school meeting successful?" Education leaders could have every aspect of a great meeting—a comfortable meeting location, all participants are on time, the lighting and acoustics are good, people pay attention, good ideas are presented, the discussion is enthusiastic—but without proper preparation the meeting will fall far short in efficiency and in productivity of what it could have been.

To avoid making any assumptions about what preparation means and about what preparation requires, the following list itemizes many essential ingredients of proper preparation for a school council meeting or for any school meeting that seeks to be efficient and productive.

Preparation Check List

(1) All members have been contacted by phone to confirm that they know the time and location of the meeting. Contacted does not mean that a phone call was made, but there was no answer. Contacted means the person was spoken to or a message was left on a recording machine *and* receipt of the message was confirmed. Contact made in person can replace the phone call.

(2) The community, parents/guardians, faculty, staff, and students have been notified one week before the meeting. Notified is more than posting a sign in the hallway. Notified is signs, memos, announcements, and word of mouth.

(3) The members of the school council have received all information they need for the meeting one week before the meeting. This information includes committee recommendations, background data or articles on topics to be considered, minutes of the last meeting, the agenda, and any other useful materials as selected by the chair or other members of the school council.

(4) The agenda has been created and posted one week before the meeting. Posted means all teachers have a copy, local businesses and other public places posted a copy and the local cable TV system has the agenda on its community bulletin board program.

(5) All committees that were given an assignment at the most recent school council meeting have met and have taken partial or complete action on their assignment.

(6) Materials for the meeting are available—pens, pencils, paper, audiotape recorder, video camera (if desired) and water—people do get thirsty when they talk.

(7) The meeting room is reserved and is properly arranged. The proper arrangement enables people to look at each other, to hear each other, and to interact. This is not a courtroom or a palace.

(8) Signs are up in the school the day of the meeting directing people to the meeting location.

(9) A custodian is scheduled to be on duty and to be available at all times during the meeting.

(10) A system of quick phone calls is in place in case bad weather or other problems would cause the meeting to be postponed.

There are additional elements of preparation beyond those ten listed above. The point is clear—school council meetings that will be efficient and productive will require hours of serious preparation. There is no reason to have a meeting for which people are not prepared.

Remember: the goal of SBDM in particular and of school improvement efforts in general is not merely to have meetings. The goal is to build consensus for decisions that will improve our school and to assign duties for implementation of those decisions.

> The point is clear—school council meetings that will be efficient and productive will require hours of serious preparation. There is no reason to have a meeting for which people are not prepared.

INFORMATION

Are people tired yet of hearing "We live in an information (a) age, (b) economy, (c) world or (d) society"? We can get information instantly. We can get information from books, discs, CD-ROMs, audiotapes, cassette tapes, voice mail, phones, e-mail, and occasional face-to-face conversations.

When we listen to the broadcast of a baseball game, the announcer could easily use computer data to help report, "John Lindsley takes strike one, making the count one ball and one strike. In his seven-year career, John has had 217 times when the count was one and one. He has gotten on base in forty-nine of those situations, but he was twice hit by the next pitch, so maybe he needs to be careful now." Should baseball broadcasts be information overloads?

The reality is that modern society has created a mammoth amount of information. Another reality is that some of the information is useless. The task of a school council in terms of information is to separate the useful from the useless. How is this done? Here's a hint—what is the purpose of school-based decision making? To make decisions, to build support for those decisions and to assign duties for implementing those decisions.

So, the useful information will be that which helps people build consensus for decisions that will improve their school. If the school council is going to consider the need of hiring a full time school security guard to help with school discipline, it is not necessary to read every available study on law enforcement. It is necessary to know if the budget can absorb a new employee, if other schools have found that this action has helped solve problems of school violence or of their school misbehavior and to know what the people associated with our school think about this proposal.

COMMITTEES

For every problem there is an equal and opposite solution. For every problem in any school there is a solution that has been tried at another school. For people who seek to improve schools through effective meetings, one tool available is the use of applicable information. The education profession publishes hundreds of periodicals, hundreds of dissertations, thousands of books and holds thousands of conferences or workshops annually. The good news is that in education we know what works. Much time is spent talking about school problems, but much effort is invested in creating, implementing and analyzing school solutions. School councils that improve schools will have meetings that include presentation of precise recommendations that are based on reliable information that has been read by, contemplated by, and analyzed by committees that report to the school council. Great school councils need a solid committee system.

"Good afternoon. Thanks for being here on time so we can get our faculty meeting started promptly. First, we need everyone to sign up for a committee."

"No. Anything but a committee, I'll supervise the cafeteria. I'll supervise the bus area. I'll clean gum off desks. Please, don't make me serve on a committee."

The principal who hears teachers beg that they be excused from committee duty is probably hearing genuine expressions of frustrations. Committee work has a reputation similar to the flu—nobody wants it, it makes you feel bad, and it seems to linger. Still, members of the school council cannot be expected to spontaneously create every brilliant solution to every problem or topic they consider at a meeting. Plus, committees can involve teachers, students, staff members, parents, and citizens who are not on the school council, but who need to be part of the successful implementation of ideas that will improve our school.

Every school and every school council needs to create a committee system so topics can be thoroughly researched, discussed and refined. The committees will be expected to make recommendations to the school council. The council may accept, change, or reject the recommendation of a committee, but the council members themselves cannot find the time or the human resources to research every topic and to identify proposed actions on every topic.

What committees need to be established? Begin with the key areas of authority given to a school council. If the council has authority for curriculum, it will be helpful to have a curriculum committee. Some common committees that may apply to many schools are listed below:

- budget
- school climate
- professional development
- community, parent, and school relations
- technology
- academics/curriculum

There are, of course, dozens of other topics that committees will deal with, but the effective committee system needs to keep the total number of separate committees to a manageable number. Discipline matters, for example, could be assigned to the school climate committee. Rewarding successful or improving students would be the work of the academics/curriculum committee.

Some ad hoc committees may be necessary occasionally. The school council may create a temporary committee to review the work of the school council itself. Ad hoc committees could be formed to help interview candidates for positions at the school if such involvement in interviewing is part of the school council's duty. If the school district's superintendent tells all principals that within one month a list of each school building's repair, maintenance and renovation priorities is due, a temporary committee could do this work and then disband after making a report to the school council.

> Attending meetings does not necessarily frustrate people. Attending meetings that accomplish nothing will frustrate people.

If committees are going to be productive, effective, and efficient, what is necessary—preparation. The committee chair needs to apply the ten steps on page 31 for the school council chair. This sounds like work and it is work, but it also gets results. Attending meetings does not necessarily frustrate people. Attending meetings that accomplish nothing will frustrate people.

CASE STUDY #1

Consideration of a hypothetical, but believable, school council committee meeting can help reveal if the committee system works. The school climate committee is meeting to identify ways that the first day of school can be a very exciting time when all students, teachers, and staff feel welcome and get the school year started well. The chair of the committee opens the meeting, on time.

Chair: Thank you for attending the school climate committee meeting today. I know that July is a busy time, but school starts in six weeks and we need to be ready. When I spoke with each of you last week you said that you had received the material I sent, so with all of us up to date on that information, let's get to work.

    The one item on the agenda is what can we do to make the first day of school this coming year the best we've ever had? You've read about what some other schools have done and you've read the summary of what our school has done in recent years. Who has an idea?

Teacher 1: I've always liked the idea of each teacher wearing a T-shirt with "Welcome Back" or some other message, maybe "We Like Our Students" or "Our Students Are Great." I know that impressed the students when we did that a few years ago.

Parent: Good idea. I read that article about the school that used T-shirts, signs, stickers and buttons with the theme for the year, I think it was "Be the Best." They even wrote a song about being the best and had chorus students sing it in the cafeteria at lunch on the first day. Could we do that?

Teacher 2: Do we have money for T-shirts and the other supplies? Won't the budget be tight this year for what we need, much less for any extras?

Chair: Our committee has a budget of $1,000. A T-shirt for each teacher and staff member cost us $478 a few years ago and it's probably higher now. That would take half of our budget for the year.

Student: Could the teachers each pay for their own T-shirt? I'll bet some parent in the school has a business that prints shirts that could save some money. Hey, can students get these shirts, too?

Teacher 1: It's not easy getting every teacher to pay extra for anything. I just doubt that people would do that.

Student: That's awful. What's a T-shirt going to cost? Six dollars or eight dollars or something like that. Is that asking too much?

Chair: What other ideas do we have?

Parent: Could the first day of school include an assembly? The students haven't seen each other for months, so this might be good for them. It's also a time when new teachers could be introduced and the principal could welcome everyone. A student could announce something about school activities that are getting started.

Teacher 2: I really hate assemblies. Some students skip them. Other students goof off or cause trouble. Some teachers even try to get out of going to them. Is there some other way we can accomplish what you are after without having an assembly?

Student: Yeah, we could have meetings for each grade. We could use the gym, the cafeteria, the library, and maybe the parking lot. Each class could have its own mini-assembly.

Chair: OK. Let's remember our goal is to get the school year off to a great start. If any problems could come up with an assembly, the school council probably will not agree with that idea. What else is there?

Parent: Here's a thought. My company opened a new office recently. On the first day, the company president gave each employee a brand new one dollar bill. He attached a note to each one saying, "Let's team up to make a lot more of these." How about giving each student a report card on the first day with an "A" grade listed for each class. The teachers could write "Let's team up to make a lot more of these" or "This is your report card now—keep it like this."

Student: Wow. Great idea! OOPS! I know we're not supposed to evaluate ideas when they are first presented, but that one really is cool.

Chair: OK. Are we beginning to get any clear picture of what we want for the first day to include? Not yet. Well, how about everyone writing a short description of what they would like us to do on the first day of school. Take a few minutes to think and to write, then we'll each read our ideas out loud. We can see if there are some common suggestions that we can easily agree on and if some other ideas could be used, too. Let's take about three or four minutes.

[*Note:* Consensus does not just happen and decisions are not just made. The chair realized that no clear direction was emerging. The short writing activity is one way of using meeting time efficiently.]
Chair: OK. Who would like to read first? Nobody. All right, I'll start and then let's just go to my left. The first day of school could include . . .

It would violate the spirit of school-based decision making to tell the rest of what the chair said. That is not how school-based decision making works. Each school has to create the answers that best resolve its questions or the solutions which best solve its problems. If the people at a school think that the first day at school needs to be improved, they should get to work. The school council, one of its committees or a special task force can use the meeting process described here to create the best opening day ever. It will not be the best because those people were told what to do and that was done. It will be the best because people at a school built consensus for a unique plan that was decided by and which had duties assigned to people in that school and community.

PREPARATION—WHO DOES WHAT, WHEN, HOW

Reminder: school council members and committee members need to be prepared for each meeting. Helping the members prepare for the meeting means getting all necessary materials to all members one week before the meeting. Mailing the material one week before the meeting is not adequate. The members need to receive the materials one week before the meeting.

Who will take responsibility for this and how will this task get done properly? It sounds so simple—get materials to people—but much could go wrong, be forgotten, get lost, or otherwise by done poorly.

The principal of the school is in the best position to complete this responsibility for the school council. The principal has no time available for one more duty, but no person can command the resources needed for this task as the principal can.

If the school council is going to meet on Monday, August 29, each school council member must receive all materials needed to prepare for that meeting by Monday, August 22. This makes the week of August 15–19 an important time. During that week the principal and his/her secretary must obtain (1) the minutes of the last meeting; (2) all committee recommendations to be considered at the August 29 meeting; (3) relevant background materials, such as articles from professional journals dealing with topics on the August 29 agenda; (4) the agenda for the meeting; and (5) copies of memos, letters, newsletters, or other high priority information from the state department of education, the district's superintendent, the PTA, or the community.

The principal or his/her secretary will have to call people on August 15 if any parts of this meeting preparation kit are missing. By close of business on Thursday, August 18 all materials are due. The secretary's first duty on Friday, August 19, is to copy the materials, collate the materials, fill the mailing envelopes addressed to each school council member and either (1) take these to the post office or have them taken by a volunteer or (2) deliver these to the home or business of each school council member—this could also be done by a volunteer.

The principal's perspective on this must equal that of a Fortune 500 company CEO preparing for a meeting of the board of directors or a university president preparing for a meeting of the board of trustees.

For school council meetings to be taken seriously, the meeting must appear to be serious, important and very well managed. For school council meetings to be productive, all members must be thoroughly prepared. School council meetings will fail and, in turn, school-based decision making will fail if preparation is inadequate. This is true for any school-related meeting.

If principals need another example, they can talk to a local high school football coach. To prepare for a game on Friday, September 9, the coach sent someone to scout the opponent on Friday, September 2. The coach had his team meet on the morning of Saturday, September 3, to watch the film of the game the night before. Each day in practice the week of September 5–8 was devoted to preparing for the game on September 9. A full week of preparation is needed for members of a football or of a school council.

THE DECISION AGENDA

Question: list the three ingredients of a successful SBDM meeting that have been explored so far: preparation, information, and committees. What is next? It starts with "a" and refers to topics that will be considered at a meeting. Right—agenda, but not just any agenda. The goals of

```
                    School Council Meeting Agenda
                      Monday, August 29, 1994
                         7 p.m. School Library

    1.    Call to order
    2.    Approve minutes from July 25, 1994
    3.    Old business - including reports
    4.    New business
          a.    Discuss grading scale
          b.    Discuss bus area rules
          c.    Discuss math textbook adoption plan
          d.    Other
    5.    Comments from guests or audience
    6.    Adjourn
```

Figure 4.1. Regular Agenda.

school-based decision making include to make decisions and to implement decisions, so we need a decision agenda. Meetings are not held to pass time or to play pretend democracy. Meetings are held so proper decisions can be made and so great results can be obtained as the decisions are implemented.

What is a decision agenda? How is it different from a regular agenda? First, look at a typical, topical agenda (Figure 4.1). Assume that this agenda is being used by a school council that has no awareness of a decision agenda.

Now, look at a decision agenda (Figure 4.2). Some differences are easily seen at first glance, but read it carefully, please.

What are the differences between the typical, topical agenda and the decision agenda? Readers of this book need to be participatory. Readers will not be given all of the answers. Central Office is not telling educators and other reformers what to do—people involved with and concerned about a school are creating the future for their school, so they have to practice now. What are the differences between the two agendas in each of the categories listed in Figure 4.3?

The typical, topical agenda lists topics to be discussed. Decisions might get made. Decisions may be avoided. There is no connection between committee reports and actions that may occur as old business or new business items are considered. The idea seems to be that the meeting will just muddle along until the group decides to adjourn.

The decision agenda is more detailed, more specific, more action oriented, more results oriented and clearly emphasizes (1) decisions to be

School Council Meeting: Decision Agenda
Monday, August 29, 1994
7:00 p.m. - 8:30 p.m.
School Library
Visitors Welcome!

	Topic	Person Responsible	Decision(s) Required
1.	Call to Order - 7:00 p.m.	Chair - Ms. Dysart	None
2.	Approve July 25 minutes	Vice-chair - Mr. Buckner	Approval
3.	Old Business - Reports		
a.	Personnel	Chair - Ms. Dysart	Select members for committee to interview candidates for new counselor; assign duties
b.	Budget	Treasurer - Ms. Franklin	Approve - or modify - accounting procedures for fund-raising events; assign duties
4.	New Business		
a.	Grading Scale	Curriculum Committee Chair Mr. Phipps	Approve, modify or reject committee recommendation; assign duties
b.	Bus Area Rules	School Climate Committee Chair - Ms. Monet	Approve, modify or reject committee recommendations; assign duties
c.	Math Textbooks	Curriculum Committee Chair - Mr. Phipps	Approve, modify or reject committee recommendations; assign duties
5.	Other • from members • from guests or audience	Chair - Ms. Dysart	Assign any topics brought up to appropriate committees
6.	Adjourn 8:30 p.m. or earlier	Chair - Ms. Dysart	

Figure 4.2. Decision Agenda.

made and (2) assignment of duties for the implementation of the decisions. The decision agenda communicates the purpose of the meeting—discussion, decision, and delegation of duties. The school council uses a committee system so recommendations are presented for approval, modification, or rejection. The committees create recommendations based on their research, discussions, and perspectives. The school council makes the final decision, but does not have to begin at "start" with each topic. The council begins with a fully developed recommendation which all school council members received one week prior to the meeting.

> The decision agenda communicates the purpose of the meeting—discussion, decision, and delegation of duties.

Which agenda takes more time and effort to prepare? The decision agenda. Remember, preparation is essential and proper preparation takes time.

Which agenda makes for a more productive and efficient meeting? The decision agenda because it leads participants towards results.

The decision agenda will not do the work for anyone. School council members still need to be prepared and informed, ready to discuss and to decide. Committees need to develop solid recommendations. The decision agenda is a meeting management tool that can help school councils do their real job, which, as is well established, is not merely to have meetings. The real job is to improve schools by having meetings that build consensus for decisions and that assign duties for implementing those decisions.

Creating a Decision Agenda

Look again at the decision agenda in Figure 4.2. Now, take a step-by-step journey through that decision agenda so the process is apparent. Each topic is followed by the decision(s) required.

Step 1: Call to order, 7:00 P.M. No decision by the school council is

Category	Differences Between the Two Agendas
Appearance	
Impression Created	
Sequence of Events	
Emphasis of The Meeting	
Likely Outcome of The Meeting	
Other	

Figure 4.3. Agenda Differences.

needed to begin the meeting; however, the council's chair must take the initiative to call the meeting to order. People will be talking socially and some people may arrive after 7:00 P.M., but to be taken seriously a school council has to act seriously and this means establishing a schedule which is followed. Note: if a quorum is not yet present, the meeting may be called to order, but no votes would be taken or no consensus decisions made until a quorum was reached.

Step 2: Approve July 25 minutes: it can be effective if this is more than a perfunctory statement of, "If there are no errors in the minutes, they stand approved." This is an opportunity to direct everyone's attention to important topics. The chair can give a one minute summary of the minutes of the last meeting. This will help the school council members remember any change(s) they noticed should be made in the minutes. This helps everyone at the meeting direct their attention to recent and current school council topics. If members will read the minutes prior to a meeting, approval could be done quickly.

Step 3: Old business

(1) Personnel—The council needs to select members for the committee that will help interview candidates for the school counselor position. First, people need to know who is eligible to serve on this committee. Second, people need to know what duties and time demands will be placed upon the members of this committee. Third, the committee needs to have some varied membership so, for example, not all members are teachers. It is good for people to volunteer to serve on an ad hoc committee such as this, but if volunteers are reluctant, the chair must appoint people and obtain their agreement to serve. Note: In Kentucky, the principal makes the decision about who is hired for school positions; however, the principal consults the school council. Using a screening committee of school council and/or committee members who make a recommendation to the principal is one good way to consult.

(2) Budget—The decision needed is to approve or to modify the accounting procedures of fundraising events and to assign duties for this accounting work. The key here is that all school council members have studied the materials they received one week before the meeting. This enables the council members to discuss the topic wisely and efficiently. The treasurer would give a short summary of the recommended accounting procedures.

Note: Before moving to the new business part of the meeting, notice that the decision agenda is not adding steps to the meeting. The decision agenda adds direction to the meeting. Participants are expected to arrive at the meeting ready to make decisions. These meetings will include discussion, but the purpose of the meeting is not to talk. The purpose of the meeting is to make decisions and to assign duties for implementing the decisions.

> The chair does not ask school council members if there are any topics that should be on the agenda for the next meeting. The chair asks, "What do we need to make decisions about at the next school council meeting?"

In setting up a decision agenda, the school council chair thinks, "What decisions do we need to make?" and "What issues need to be resolved?" The answers to these questions create the topics for the agenda. There is a difference—topics of interest do not create an agenda. The chair does not ask school council members if there are any topics which should be on the agenda for the next meeting. The chair asks, "What do we need to make decisions about at the next school council meeting?"

Step 4: New business

(1) Grading scale

(2) Bus area rules

(3) Math textbooks

In each of these cases, the decision to be made by the school council will be to approve, modify, or reject the recommendation from the committee which has discussed the topic and developed a proposal. It is essential that school council members received a copy of each proposal one week prior to the council meeting. This means that the principal must stay in close touch with the committee chairs to be sure deadlines are met. If school council members were not given the recommendation of a committee one week before the school council meeting, consideration of that committee's work must wait for the next school council meeting.

Step 5: Other
  • from members
  • from guests or audience

The challenge here is to avoid long discussions of topics that are mentioned. Do not dismiss these topics as unimportant, but expedite proper consideration of the topics by (a) assigning topics to the relevant school council committee if the school council has jurisdiction or (b) direct the person who suggested a topic to contact another person—say who that is and how they can be reached—if the school council does not have jurisdiction.

Step 6: Adjourn, 8:30 P.M. The decisions that impact this are made by the chair throughout the meeting. Those decisions are the ones which end discussion on topics so the council can make a decision and move to the next topic. It is vital to respect the schedules of school council members who need to get home or elsewhere. The meetings of a respected school council will begin on time and will end on time.

Next question: what activity will consume most of the time at a school council meeting? Is that question unclear? OK, it can be rephrased. What will people at the school council meeting do during the meeting?

They will talk and listen. The activity that will build consensus for decisions that improve our school is discussion. Of course, schools have been places of talking and listening for decades or centuries. What is new about the discussion during a school council meeting? Nothing, unless action is taken to make the discussion have more meaning and more substance than may be common.

SCHOOL PURPOSE

The action we must take initially is to answer one question. What is the purpose of the school? Purpose does not mean mission, mission statement, goals or objective. Purpose is that which is the school's reason for being. Purpose is the core, the marrow, the essence. Purpose is that which cannot be removed without causing the school to cease existing. Take away the gym, the cafeteria , the clubs, the teams and a school can still exist. Why? Because the essence, the purpose, of the school is not revealed by what is done via the gym, cafeteria, clubs or teams.

Page 9 merits a second look. Concentrate on this statement: "The purpose of a school is to cause learning." That generalized statement of school purpose needs to be applied specifically to the school which concerns the reader. The purpose of an elementary school is to cause learning. The purpose of a graduate school of law is to cause learning. The specific learning, the methods of learning and the application of learning will differ in an elementary school contrasted with a law school; however, each school's purpose begins with learning as the core and adds specific details as appropriate.

The purpose of a school, of any school, of every school, of school itself is to cause learning. The purpose of each individual school will begin with learning and will also include unique aspects associated with that particular school.

Take a few minutes and complete this sentence: "The purpose of our school is _____

_____

_____

_____."

The school council needs to agree on the statement of purpose for the school. Hundreds of people should submit their sentence, which states the purpose of the school. Using all ideas proposed, the school council committee assigned to recommend a statement of purpose will reach agreement on one clear, concise statement. The school council will consider the recommendation and will make the final decision.

What does a statement of school purpose have to do with making the discussions at a school council meeting more efficient and productive? Consider this—how could the statement of purpose help guide school council discussions so comments stay on appropriate topics and so comments help bring about effective decisions?

Every topic on the decision agenda of a school council meeting must directly relate to the school's statement of _____ (the answer is "purpose").

Every comment made during the discussions at a school council meeting must relate to the school's statement of _____ (same answer—"purpose").

If a person at the school council starts preaching a sermon which is full of their ego, their political games, their personal agenda and/or their career, the statement of purpose rule can be invoked. This could be done by the chair who holds a small sign which has the statement of purpose printed on it. This could be done by the chair simply asking the speaker, "Please explain how your comments directly relate to the school's purpose?" The chair could be more aggressive and say, "These comments are off purpose. We need to move on."

A school may prefer to give each council member the authority to object as lawyers in the courtroom do. If a comment seems to be off purpose, a school council member could object—due to the comment being off purpose, not due to the person speaking or due to whether the comment made sense. The chair could sustain the objection or could overrule it.

It is hoped that school council members would soon be in the habit of proposing topics and of making comments which are only in the purpose category. It may take longer for visitors to get in this habit, but that is part of the SBDM learning curve.

DECISIONS

How will a school council make decisions once the committee recommendation is considered and the discussion is completed? There is one word to suggest the preferred decision making method—consensus. Consensus will not always mean that every member of the school council is 100% enthusiastic about an idea: rather, all members of the council agree to be supportive of an idea and to do all they can to make the idea work. In order to reach the goal—build consensus for decisions and duties that will improve our school—we cannot endure a mentality of "my way is the only way." Improving schools is not a "my way" process. SBDM is not a "my way" process. School improvement in general and school-based decision making in particular are "our way" processes.

Taking a vote is not wrong, it is not the preference, but it is necessary sometimes. Decisions need to be made. Consensus will not always emerge. It may be helpful during a discussion to take a quick reading of the school council members. "OK, we've discussed this for ten minutes and let's just see where we are." At that point the chair could ask each member to state his or her current thought about the recommendation. The chair may say, "Who is in favor? Who is against?" The chair could, showing some deference to the committee system, say, "We've discussed this enough. Is there any opposition to the recommendation?" The dynamics are a bit different if the chair asks, "Are we all in favor of this?"

Do not be afraid to send a recommendation back to the committee for additional work. "There really is no consensus yet. You've heard the questions and comments about their recommendation. Please have your committee revise the recommendation accommodating the thoughts you've heard at this meeting as much as possible. We'll consider your revision at the next school council meeting."

We can put the ideal decision making process into an equation, such as shown in Figure 4.4.

We can also put the ideal decision making process into a flow chart which flows from bottom up as shown in Figure 4.5.

Statement of purpose	+ Well developed recommendations consistent with the purpose + Preparation, information, decision agenda, discussion

= Efficiently made decisions, usually by consensus.

Figure 4.4. Decision Making Equation.

6.	Follow up by the Principal and status reports given at future School Council meetings until implementation of a decision is completed.	
5.	Decisions made by the School Council and implementation duties assigned to individuals.	5.a. The School Council may decide to send a recommendation back for more committee work.
4.	School Council meeting structured according to a Decision Agenda.	
3.	• School Council members read the material they received one week before a meeting. • Confirm that school council members will attend the meeting. • Publicize the meeting and the agenda.	
2.	Well developed recommendations prepared by committees for school council consideration.	
1.	Statement of school purpose.	

Figure 4.5. Decision Making Process.

More Communication

The good news is that the process for preparing for and managing effective, efficient and productive SBDM meetings is known, along with the process of reaching decisions. After decisions are made they need to be communicated. How will this be done? Take a minute and list all the ways for the school council to communicate its decisions to all groups in the school and in the school community.

Ways to communicate school council decisions:

(1)

(2)

(3)

(4)

(5)

(6)

(7)

(8)

(9)

(10)

A list may include ideas such as: distribute minutes of the meeting, include the meeting summary in PTA newsletter, send summary of meeting to local newspaper, make PA announcement about decisions made, have the school council meeting filmed and broadcast on cable TV local access or place a story about the meeting in the school newspaper.

Could there be a contest so students who can list all SBDM decisions at the last meeting get bonus points on a Social Studies quiz? Could people put their list of all SBDM decisions on paper and put it in the box in the office. Then ten lists are drawn and each complete, correct list earns free admission to the next school event.

How do teachers, students, parents and community get information? Ask those people what they read, watch and listen to. Get information about the school council in or on those media.

There is much more to know and to do, but progress is being made. Preparation, information, committees, the decision agenda, recommendations, statement of purpose, discussion, decision making, and communication have been considered. It is clear how to make sure that everyone on the school council knows all of this. Ways of helping other people—students, teachers, parents, guardians, and community members—learn more about SBDM and become involved with a school council have been identified. People who would have meetings that improve schools must confront the reality that problems occur, mistakes are made and disasters happen. The next topic is to find ways to minimize or prevent some of these likely difficulties.

"I Wish We Had That Meeting to Do Over"

Using another case study, Chapter 5 explores predictable mistakes and problems in meetings. The reader will increasingly become an active participant in the process of creating a productive meeting. The Decision Agenda will be used to bring order, direction and efficiency to the potentially chaotic or inefficient processes of democracy. The case study will conclude with a meeting that avoids predictable mistakes and problems.

"That meeting was a waste of time. We got nowhere. I should have walked out."

"Well, at least you were already at school. The parents had to make an extra trip to come, plus I had to hire a babysitter. I can't be a school reformer and a parent if the meetings are this frustrating."

Those comments could be made by far too many teachers or parents following far too many school meetings. It would not be possible to create a meeting which produces decisions that satisfy everyone. Whenever one decision is made, other options are rejected.

The process of meetings can be enhanced so all participants or constituents can believe that decisions were made in a fair, reasonable, rational, open and democratic way which justified their effort.

Even with the best possible process, some people will complain. People will claim that their opinion was not sought, that their concerns were ignored or that their ideas were rejected. Some people will complain because their life is dedicated to finding fault, not to finding solutions.

Even with the best possible process, people who participate in meetings will bring their ego, their personal agenda, their ulterior motives, their dislike of other participants, their deal-making plans and their turf protection strategies. The best process is still going to involve imperfect people, but the pursuit of better schools is worth the effort. The current process used in too many school meetings is inadequate, so any possible corrections should be made.

To be specific about school-based decision making, what are the predictable problems associated with school council meetings and how can we prevent them or deal with them? To answer these questions, a script of one school council meeting will be reviewed. While reading the script, think, "How could this meeting be improved?" Be ready soon to consider improvements and to create a script of a much better meeting.

It is reasonable to ask, "Why can't experts just tell the people at any school how to conduct a meeting? Why can't those experts just tell those people the problems to expect and how to solve them?"

The answer to those questions is probably obvious. Meetings that improve schools in general and school-based decision making meetings in particular, are not parts of a process of people being told how to improve their school. The process is one of people obtaining all helpful information and then inventing their ways to improve their school. Making the process of school-based decision making succeed at a school is up to as many people as possible associated with that school sharing responsibility. It is prudent to team up right now and to practice some shared responsibility.

CASE STUDY #2

(1) School council meeting: Monday, September 26, 4:00 P.M.
(2) School council members (the list will expand this time to include a classified employee and a student):
- Ms. Armstrong, principal
- Mr. Johnson, teacher
- Mr. Williams, teacher
- Ms. Sullivan, teacher
- Ms. Thompson, parent
- Dr. Shepherd, parent
- Mr. Lowery, classified staff member
- Ms. Hopkins, student

(3) Agenda:
- minutes of August meeting
- tardy policy
- dress code: (a) students, (b) teachers
- violence at school
- student failure rate
- other topics
- adjourn

Ms. Armstrong: Well, it's already a few minutes after 4, so let's start. We have a quorum and the other members may arrive late. Were there any changes for the minutes of the August meeting?

Ms. Thompson: I did not receive a copy of the minutes. Did everyone else?

Dr. Shepherd: I did not receive a copy, either.

Ms. Armstrong: I know that the teachers got their copy because I put them in their mailboxes. Same with the copies for our student and staff member. I'm sorry. I guess we did not mail the copies to parents. Here's an extra for the two of you to share. Did everyone else think that the minutes were OK? If there is no objection, we'll approve those.

    The first topic on the agenda is the tardy policy. We discussed this last month, but took no action because we wanted to see if the tardy problem was as bad this year as last year. As you know, we require students to be at school and in class by 8:00 each morning. They are required to be in their seat when the bell rings for each class. Our policy has been that with three tardies you have to attend Saturday school, which is from 9:00 until noon. With three more tardies you are suspended from school for two days or your parent/guardian attends school with you for two full days. If there are more tardies after that, we suspend you one day for each tardy. The tardies accumulate for one semester and then we start over with the next semester.

    We're discussing this today because our counselors asked us to. They are not here, but the teacher representatives may be able to speak for them.

Ms. Sullivan: I spoke with both counselors today. What they want is an alternative to suspension. They want some in-school program that these tardy students are assigned to for as long as it takes to solve the problem.

Ms. Thompson: Do we know why students are tardy?

Mr. Lowery: I see them all over the building when they have a class change. The younger ones and the older ones will try to hide in places. I guess they think they won't get caught.

Ms. Hopkins: Most students are on time. The students who are always tardy probably don't care about school and don't care what you do to them.

Mr. Johnson: Sure, we know why students are tardy. Nobody ever made them follow rules in their whole lives. We suspend them and they get to watch TV at home. The counselors have a good idea. If you are late to class, you don't get to go into the class. You get put in an in-school program that isolates you and that makes you do more work than you usually do.

Mr. Williams: I wonder if some of the students who are always tardy are trying to tell us that something is wrong in their lives.

Mr. Johnson: What's wrong is that they are out of control. They've been allowed to run wild forever.

Ms. Thompson: I've heard that some teachers never have a problem with students being tardy. Those teachers seem to be able to get respect and cooperation. Why aren't all teachers able to enforce this rule the same way?

Ms. Hopkins: Some teachers kind of overlook it. The rule is that students are in the seat when the bell rings, but some teachers let it go. If you run in right after the bell they don't care! I heard one say that putting up with tardies was less trouble than filling out forms about who was tardy.

Mr. Lowery: I've heard teachers talk about this in the lounge at lunch. One said that he was usually late to school himself, so it didn't bother him to have students come late. He seemed to think that the tardy process was just a joke.

Ms. Armstrong: Well let's not get too personal on this. I guess we could talk about this all day and not get anywhere. Any ideas?

Dr. Shepherd: The counselors have real concerns about this and they did offer an idea. Could we ask them to develop a revised tardy plan? They could present it at our next meeting.

Ms. Armstrong: Is that OK? Good. I'll talk to the counselors this week about that. Our next topic is the idea of a dress code, actually two dress codes, one for students and one for teachers. Who wanted this on the agenda? Ms. Thompson, OK, you start us off, please.

Ms. Thompson: I try to spend time each week at the school. I visit classes, I help in the office, and I just volunteer where I can be helpful. I think the students are too casual in their dress, but the teachers are just as casual. I'd like to see if we can dress with the idea that we are coming to school to get some work done. It looks like people are here for social pleasures on most days.

Ms. Williams: I wonder if how people dress really matters much. If you aren't comfortable, it is hard to work.

Ms. Thompson: If you are too comfortable you never work. School is work. I know that we are not going to put people in uniforms or in battle fatigues, but let's get serious. Teachers in sweatsuits, teachers in T-shirts, students with skimpy tops or super short shorts, what good do these outfits do us? Maybe uniforms are a good idea.

Ms. Hopkins: Some students are just trying to see what they can get away with. The dress code is so vague now that students can always say that there is no rule against what they are wearing.

Ms. Thompson: Are there any limits at all now?

Ms. Armstrong: Of course. Nothing that disrupts the proper educational process can be worn. We don't analyze each student as they come in each morning to inspect their clothes. If someone notices a problem or reports a problem, we deal with it. Ms. Thompson, what do you think the dress code should require?

Ms. Thompson: Let's start with teachers. The men need to quit wearing their golf clothes. They should wear dress shirts with a tie, long pants, and some shoes that are for work, not for basketball. The women teachers need to dress as they would if they worked in a bank or in any office. Appropriate dresses, skirt, and blouse outfits or pants outfits. The students need to quit wearing party clothes. Why are shorts necessary? Why are hats necessary? Why are huge coats necessary—who knows what is hidden in them or stolen and stuffed in them. Why are some suggestive styles or crude printed designs and words allowed?

Dr. Shepherd: We could discuss styles and personal freedom and dress for success forever. People disagree on this. Since Ms. Thompson seems to be most concerned about the dress code, could she write a new dress code and share that with us next month?

Ms. Armstrong: Well, next month will be the time we discuss the tardy proposal. Could we deal with the dress code in November?

Ms. Thompson: I hate to wait so long. By November the year is almost half over. I can be ready in October.

Ms. Armstrong: Well, we'll put it on the October agenda, but if we don't get to it then, we'll have to wait until November. Now, the PTA has asked us to discuss the topic of violence at school. Ms. Thompson, you're the PTA vice-president, maybe you can tell us exactly what your group has in mind.

Ms. Thompson: We hear all of the news reports about students of all ages bringing weapons to school or about teachers being assaulted. We hear the stories or the rumors of students who feel scared to go to a bathroom because someone will steal their money or their coat. We just want to find out what is really going on at our school and what needs to be done.

Mr. Lowery: That is true. My staff keeps the bathroom clean all day. We see students in there threatening each other. We run them out, but later on you'll see it happen again. I think we need some police officers here all day.

Ms. Sullivan: I've heard teachers say that they won't come in the school alone. They wait in their car until another teacher arrives. Same when they leave. I know that some teachers will never come for any event at night because they are afraid.

Mr. Williams: This is going on everywhere. Elementary schools, middle schools, and high schools are feeling the violence of our society. I wonder if some of the violent students are trying to tell us that something is wrong in their lives.

Mr. Johnson: Yeah, something is wrong. They are crazy. Their home life is crazy. We make excuses for them. The violent students are creating chaos for the 98% of students who get along and who cooperate. We need to send the violent ones to places that are twenty-four hours per day, seven days a week. They need to be in a combination prison and school.

Dr. Shepherd: That could work, but this school council is not going to be able to create a new institution like that. What is the violence problem here? Does anyone know exactly what we are dealing with here?

Ms. Hopkins: Sure. There are some guns and knives here every day. There are some drug deals. There is a lot of stealing. Maybe 5% of the students are responsible for this. The fights at school are usually over some problem that started the night before or the weekend before.

Dr. Shepherd: So, what do we do about it? Ms. Armstrong, what are other schools doing?

Ms. Armstrong: I'd have to check some educational journals to read up on that. I don't think our school is a war zone. The problems we have in these areas are dealt with according to our rules or policies. We've had no more fights or suspensions this year that we had at the start of last year.

Dr. Shepherd: Well, that does not show any progress. We're as good or as bad as last year, but we aren't any better. Ms. Thompson, what does the PTA want us to do?

Ms. Thompson: Make sure that school is safe.

Dr. Shepherd: I know that. How does the PTA expect that to happen? Can't parents and guardians accept a lot of the responsibility? The school can help, but the families are a big part of the solution.

Ms. Thompson: That is true. I've heard that at school some teachers never have a problem with students being violent in their classrooms or in any area they supervise. Other teachers seem to invite misbehavior or violence because they cannot control students. That's another part of this problem.

Ms. Hopkins: It's like tardies or the dress code. Students have the system figured out. We know which teachers will enforce rules and which ones won't. We know what will get punished and what won't.

Ms. Armstrong: Well, violence could be discussed forever. We need the PTA to get more specific and let us know the exact problem. I still think that this school is doing OK about being a safe place. If the PTA can get more specific, we'll deal with any suggestion they have. Is that OK, Ms. Thompson?

Ms. Thompson: At the next PTA meeting, I'll ask for more information and then let you know.

Ms. Armstrong: We're supposed to discuss the student failure rate. I'm told that teachers are already concerned that more students are just not completing work this year. The teachers predict more failures this year than before.

Ms. Thompson: I've heard that some teachers give a "D" grade even when the student does no work. The teachers just don't want to deal with the effort they have to make to get everyone to work.

Mr. Williams: I wonder if some of the students who are always failing at school are trying to tell us that something is wrong in their lives.

Ms. Sullivan: I get tired of Ms. Thompson always telling us what she has heard about some teachers. We hear some awful stories about parents, but we don't bring that up at a school council meeting. And Mr. Williams, why do you always think that these students are trying to send us signals by being tardy or violent or failing. Face the facts, some of these students are getting away with being jerks and you shouldn't make excuses for them.

Ms. Armstrong: Wait a minute. We aren't here to blame each other or to get personal. We can discuss topics, not people. Is there any other discussion about students who are failing? No, OK, well, I'll ask the counselors to get more information after report cards come out in October. We'll know more then. It's getting late. Unless there are urgent topics, maybe we should adjourn.

Ms. Thompson: I know we can't get personal, but one PTA member asked me to tell you that she heard of a teacher being seen at the drive-in movies with some students.

Ms. Armstrong: Come on, we deal with topics, not with individuals or rumors. If there are no objections, the meeting is adjourned.

How could that meeting be improved? Think in terms of the organization of the meeting, the content of the meeting and the management of the meeting. What was accomplished? How could more have been accomplished? What problems caused the meeting to be inefficient or unproductive? How could those problems have been prevented or resolved? How could some members of the school council be guided so their contribution to the meeting is more useful?

Please write some ideas and then be prepared to create a better meeting.

Actions that could be taken to improve the school council meeting:

(1)

(2)

(3)

(4)

(5)

(6)

(7)

(8)

Keep thinking, please. Come up with two more suggestions, then a list of suggestions will be provided to add to items 1–10.

(9)

(10)

Keen's list of improvements:

(11) Start the meeting at a later time so it is more convenient for working parents or community members to attend.

(12) Have a time set for the start of the meeting and a time set for the conclusion.

(13) Use a decision agenda instead of the typical, topical agenda.

(14) Make sure that all members get the minutes of the prior meeting.

(15) Every topic on the agenda must have a recommendation for the school council to consider. Each recommendation was developed by a school council committee and was provided to school council members one week prior to the meeting at which the recommendation will be considered.

(16) All school council members received, one week in advance, appropriate data related to agenda items such as (a) copies of the tardy policy and the dress code and (b) statistics about school violence and the student failure rate.

(17) Have a statement of purpose for the school so all discussion during the school council meeting can be directed toward that statement or can be declared to be "off-purpose."

(18) Before school council members begin their duties, they need to have thorough training in what their job is, in how to do that job and in how to conduct meetings that improve schools.

A better meeting can be created. Please write the agenda using the partial information in Figure 5.1 as a start. Use the same people and topics from the previous script.

School Council Meeting: Decision Agenda

Monday, September 26

6:30 p.m. - 8:00 p.m.

Room 117

Visitors Welcome

	Topic	Person Responsible	Decision Required Now
1.	Call to Order		
2.	Approve August minutes		
3.	Old Business - Reports		
a.	Tardy Policy		
b.			
4.	New Business		
a.	Dress Code		
	1. Students		
	2. Teachers		
b.	Violence at School		
c.	Student Failure Rate		
5.	Other • from members • from guests or audience		
6.	Adjourn 8:00 p.m. or earlier		

Figure 5.1. *Decision Agenda Completion Activity.*

CASE STUDY #2, REVISED

Now, write the script. The script for items 1, 2, 3, and 5 is provided, but add improvements to those parts whenever possible. The script for item 4 needs to be written. Don't leave those pages blank—write!

OK, the script for the first topic under item 4 will be provided, also. The dress code topic portion of the script is provided, but the script for violence at school, student failure and other topics needs to be written.

Please incorporate as many of the ideas listed on pages 58 to 59 for improving the meeting as possible. This new script of the better meeting should be what an SBDM meeting is ideally!

Ms. Armstrong: Good evening. It is 6:30 P.M. exactly. Thanks for being here on time. When we called or spoke at school last week to confirm your attendance, you each said that you had received the minutes of the August meeting and had read them along with the other materials that were sent. Are there any changes in those minutes? None, OK, they are approved.

Under old business, we have a revised recommendation for the tardy policy. At the August meeting we discussed the recommendation from our counselors who had worked with the school climate committee. The counselors and that committee took the school council's input and created a new recommendation. Each of you received that a week ago at school or in the mail. Are there any comments?

Ms. Thompson: I was pleased to see that the revised recommendation includes a quarterly review of tardies according to each teacher and each class. This way we will know if students are tardy without regard to class or if they pick and choose some classes to be tardy to because they think the teacher in those classes won't care. Of course, dealing with those teachers would be up to the principal, not us.

Mr. Williams: I agree with the punishments for tardies, but the best idea is that after eight tardies a student has to have a conference with a counselor and the parent or guardian has to attend.

Ms. Sullivan: The biggest part of this recommendation is that our attendance clerk will be able to help supervise the in-school detention program. The PTA has agreed to provide two hours each day of volunteer work to do the most essential attendance record keeping and the one teacher who had an extra planning period will pick up some other attendance keeping duties. I'm all for it, but we need to review it at the end of the first semester to be sure that the plan is working.

Mr. Thompson: A student has a conference with a counselor and his or her parent after eight tardies. Won't this put a big time demand on the counselors?

Ms. Armstrong: After four tardies, the student goes to the in-school detention room for two full days. We hope that prevents many more tardies. If we need to change this we can at the end of the first semester. At least this gets us started.

Ms. Hopkins: I've heard students say that they will just skip a full day of school if they think they will be late getting here.

Ms. Armstrong: We'll have to make sure that we check every absence and see who is skipping. That's a good point. We seem to support the revised recommendation. Four tardies means two days of in-school detention and notification to the parent or guardian. Eight tardies means the conference with parent, counselor and student. For each tardy after that, the student is suspended out of school for one day or the student is accompanied all day at school by a parent or guardian. We'll evaluate this at the end of the first semester. The new policy would begin next Monday with each student having a clean slate of zero tardies and at the start of the second semester we'll give every student a clean slate again. We seem to have consensus on this. Any objection? No? Good. Any other old business? No, OK, let's move to new business. Ms. Thompson and the school climate committee have prepared their dress code recommendation, which everyone received one week ago. Ms. Thompson, please summarize the committee's recommendation.

Ms. Thompson: We met with the school board attorney, the president of the county teachers association and the school's student council officers. What we have recommended is consistent with law and with school board policies. For teachers, the standard is to dress as a professional. Men will wear dress shirts and a tie, dress pants and non-athletic shoes. A sport coat or a suit would not be required, but are certainly common in some other professions. Gym or physical education teachers, men or women, may dress appropriately for their work. The same is true for vocational education teachers. Women will wear dresses, skirt and blouse coordinates, pant outfits, or coordinated suits. No athletic shoes, although comfortable dress shoes are fine. No sweatsuits, even the very expensive, stylish ones for women or men.

Of course, we say teachers, but we mean all adult staff members except the maintenance crew, the cafeteria staff or school nurse.

For students, the standard is to dress for school, not for a party. Long pants are preferred, although shorts that are knee length are allowed. Shirts are full length and are buttoned properly. T-shirts are allowed, but they cannot be see through and neither can other shirts or blouses. No clothes can communicate any message or idea that is vulgar, discriminatory, or that could incite a fight. There are some other details that you've read, so I won't list them all now.

Ms. Hopkins: Students are really mad about this because it is September. Everyone has their clothes for this year. We can't change now and go buy new clothes. Maybe this plan could start next year.

Mr. Johnson: Students aren't half as mad as the teachers are. The teachers I've heard from are threatening to sue the school council over this. Lots of them planned to attend tonight, but they hoped we could work it out for them without having to stage a huge protest.

Dr. Shepherd: What is the problem with having people dress in a way that says they are serious about the work they have to do. If teachers come to work looking like they are on vacation, who can take them seriously! If students come to school looking like they are ready for a party, is it any wonder that they are tardy or that they fail or that they get violent?

Mr. Lowery: Did we ever consider a uniform? Every student wears a blue shirt and blue pants. That means parents don't have to listen to the students ask for the latest style. It might also cut down on stealing or fighting—they steal clothes from each other now and they fight over comments about how they dress.

Ms. Thompson: Our committee takes the dress code recommendation seriously. We thought there was general agreement that people in this school were dressing too casually. We intentionally avoided the uniform idea so people could still have some choices. What should we do now?

Ms. Armstrong: We don't have consensus on this. Just to get an accurate feel for your thoughts, how many of you could support the recommendation now? Three of you. Well, that won't work. Do you think the School Climate committee should take a survey or do we just drop this?

Dr. Shepherd: Let's not give up, yet. Take the survey of teachers and students. Tell them we will have a dress code and they have to accept that. Tell them the goal of the dress code is to help create an attitude that at school we are serious about our work. We could get input from parents and the community, too. We probably have to delay the new dress code until the next school year, but let's get it agreed to and communicated this year.

Ms. Armstrong: That sounds reasonable. If there are no objections, we will ask the school climate committee to complete those surveys in October and to present a new recommendation to us in November. Ms. Thompson, thank you for your work and for your patience.

Our next topic is violence at school. This topic was discussed recently at a PTA meeting. Ms. Thompson, you're a busy person today. As PTA Vice-President, please tell us what your group and the school climate committee are recommending that the school council should do.

Note: Write the script for this issue. Try to include all school council members. Be sure to reach a decision. The blank lines at the left are where the name of the person who is speaking is put. Please, use other paper if this book was borrowed.

Ms. Thompson: _____

_____

_____

_____

_____

_____: _____

_____

_____

_____

_____: _____

_____

_____

_____

_____: _____

_____

_____

_____

_____: _____

_____

_____

_____

_____: _____

_____

_____

_____ : _____
_____
_____
_____
_____
_____
_____
_____
_____ : _____
_____
_____
_____
_____
_____
_____
_____ : _____
_____
_____
_____
_____
_____
_____ : _____
_____
_____
_____
_____

Note: Good job. Ready to try again? The next topic is the student failure rate.

Ms. Armstrong: OK, now we'll discuss the topic of students who are failing at school.

_____ : _____
_____
_____
_____
_____
_____ : _____
_____
_____
_____
_____
_____ : _____

_____
_____
_____
_____
_____
_____ : _____
_____
_____
_____
_____
_____
_____ : _____
_____
_____
_____
_____
_____
_____ : _____
_____
_____
_____
_____
_____
_____ : _____
_____
_____
_____
_____
_____
_____ : _____
_____
_____
_____
_____

Note: As promised, the rest of the script for this meeting is provided; however, please write ideas in the margin or elsewhere; however, if this book was borrowed, use other paper for notes.

Ms. Armstrong: It is about ten minutes until eight. We have some time for other comments from guests or from school council members before we adjourn at eight.

Ms. Thompson: I have a question about procedures. Our committee had two meetings when we discussed the proposals for dress codes.

Teachers and students were invited to attend those committee meetings, but the only people who came were the members of our committee. It took a lot of time and a lot of work to get the recommendations ready. At tonight's meeting we got criticized and our recommendation was rejected. Now we have to spend time taking surveys and writing new recommendations. We could work on this during the next two months and still the school council could reject it in November. Can you see why I am frustrated?

Ms. Armstrong: All I can tell you is that the process of a school council making a decision can be slow and frustrating. School-based decision making gives committees or individuals the power to recommend, but the full school council has the power to approve, to reject or to change any recommendations. I'd ask you to hang in there and work with our process.

Ms. Thompson: OK, but maybe our by-laws could be changed so a unanimous committee recommendation, like we had on the dress codes, can be defeated only with a three-fourths vote of the school council. That means six of the members instead of five now for a simple majority.

Ms. Armstrong: If you would like the by-laws committee to consider that, I'd encourage you to talk to Dr. Shepherd—he's that committee's chair. Any other topics?

Mr. Johnson: Explain to me again if I am supposed to speak and to vote at these meetings as most teachers tell me to or as I think is right?

Ms. Armstrong: That's the oldest question in any representative democracy. You won the election. A majority of teachers must trust you and your ideas. Keep in very close touch with the teachers, they are your constituents. You can't vote to please all of them because they are not always in complete agreement with each other. You can represent their thoughts for them, even if that means you tell us about the different opinions of different teachers on the same subject. Get all the information you can and hear from all the teachers you can, then check the school's statement of purpose and vote accordingly. It is 8:00 P.M. and we need to conclude. OK? With your agreement, we are adjourned. Thank you for your time tonight.

(1) Did the revised meeting build consensus?
(2) Did the revised meeting make decisions?
(3) Will those decisions improve the school?

(4) Did the revised meeting have:
- start and stop times
- a decision agenda
- recommendations to consider
- materials sent to school council meetings one week ahead of the meeting
- comments on topics not on people or on personalities
- assignments of duties for the implementation of each decision
- other requirements of meetings that improve schools, such as:

  1.

  2.

  3.

The concept of school-based decision making is partly idealistic. It is idealistic to think that administrators, teachers, staff members, parents or guardians, community members and students will listen to each other, reason together, make decisions, accept duties for implementing those decisions, and do all of this with no compensation for their school council work.

Would it be better if the principal autocratically made every decision and assigned duties for implementation? Democracy is slow and frustrating, but it can be vibrant, inspiring and productive. Democracy can create an atmosphere of "we are in this together" and that atmosphere of trust, mutual concern and mutual commitment can make a school thrive.

School-based decision making enables us to have a process which, through productive meetings, can improve schools. By improving schools we can cause learning to occur in the life of each student in ways which are better in quality and in quantity than that which has existed. Sure, SBDM is idealistic, but so is the concept of education. The two ideals—democratic, decentralized, participatory management and education—are symbiotic.

Still, those ideals clash with the reality of politics, ego, personality clashes, hidden motives, too much to do in too little time and the fact that working to improve schools now is a difficult task. Such realities must now be addressed.

Realities

The best plan for a productive meeting, a carefully prepared Decision Agenda and a brilliant statement of school purpose can still run into a relentless force which seeks to undermine the effort to improve schools—the peopleness of people. Motives, emotions, power struggles, animosity, prejudice and other human realities come to meetings with the people in attendance. School is not the top priority of everyone employed at, concerned with or impacted by a school. Chapter 6 addresses realities that must be dealt with to most completely improve schools.

Too long. Not long enough. Too many people. Not enough people for a quorum. Too loud and noisy. It was difficult to hear the speakers. People got off the subject. My topic never came up. The room was too hot. The seats were uncomfortable.

The list of complaints about meetings is lengthy. Some of the complaints are valid and corrections can be made. Some of the complaints are about situations that are impossible to correct. Some complaints come from those who are chronic complainers.

Still, there are realistic, procedural or logistical problems which can undermine a meeting. In the dynamic adventure of improving schools, the people who are responsible for meetings can anticipate realistic problems and can prevent some of those problems while being ready to confront the problems which are inevitable.

TIME MANAGEMENT

Somewhere between the start of the 1950s and the end of the 1960s life got so busy that time management became an essential skill for children and adults. Schools are already time sensitive places where bells ring, schedules are established and tardiness is punished.

Are there any pockets of time during a school day which could be made more productive? Could teachers have a weekly working lunch to replace an after school meeting? Could some parents attend a meeting before school rather than in the evening? How about a Super Saturday School where teachers, parents and community members meet while children and teenagers use the gym, computer lab and library under parental supervision? Could a conference phone call replace some preliminary meetings? The empty school schedule of summer could be an opportunity.

People find time for priorities. Getting creative in uses of time for scheduling meetings may make meetings more appealing.

NOBODY VOLUNTEERS TO KEEP MINUTES OF THE MEETING

Take turns. A different person does this task at each meeting until everyone has had a turn, then start over. Put everyone's name on separate slips of paper. Put the slips into a box. The name drawn takes notes of today's meeting. The second name drawn takes notes next time.

Audiotape and videotape the meeting. Perhaps these could replace detailed written minutes or make a very short written summary acceptable if combined with the tape of the meeting.

PEOPLE MAKE CRITICAL COMMENTS ABOUT OTHER PEOPLE

How are students treated when they are critical of each other? They are punished after being told not to tease, make fun of, gossip about, or criticize other people.

Adult participants in meetings that improve schools need to be guided by the meeting leader in rules such as to discuss ideas, not people; disagree over ideas, not people; challenge ideas, not people.

PARTICIPATION IN VOTING

When teachers vote on the faculty members who will represent them on the school council, it is likely that teacher participation in the election will be very high, perhaps 100%. This election will probably occur one day right after school, thus making it convenient for all teachers to participate.

There is no equally convenient time for the election which will be held to select parent/guardian members or community members of the school council. If this election is in the afternoon on Monday through Friday, it will conflict with the employment schedule of many adults. An evening election will be difficult for single parents and for people who work nights. An election on the weekend conflicts with family activities. Having the election at the school may cause problems for adults who do not have a car or other convenient transportation.

The Kentucky experience indicates that in most schools the percentage of parents/guardians participating in these elections has been quite low, in some cases only about 5%. There are many reasons and few perfect solutions, but some ideas may help.

(1) Schedule the election on the night of a major event at school—a concert, sports activity, open house, or social event.

(2) Conduct the election from 8 A.M. through 8 P.M. The school's office is open 8 A.M. through about 4 P.M. anyway, so volunteers are needed from 4 P.M. to 8 P.M. only.

(3) Permit people to vote through the mail as is done in absentee balloting. Some restrictions would need to be used to avoid fraud. The school board lawyer and local or state election officials could help structure this.

(4) Have voting locations throughout the school's attendance area, perhaps at shopping centers.

(5) Have a mobile voting booth which goes throughout the school's attendance area in a van or recreational vehicle.

(6) Conduct the election on the same day that the city, county, or state is having a primary or general election. Use the same precincts where people will go vote for mayor, governor, or other races, but have a separate ballot, unless school attendance boundaries are the same as precinct boundaries.

(7) Is there a way to permit voting by fax without having fraud? If so, try that.

(8) Think of another idea: _____

_____

DO I VOTE MY OPINION OR MY CONSTITUENTS' OPINION?

This has been debated for centuries as representative government has progressed. I once asked a member of the U.S. House of Representatives how he resolved this matter. He said, "I vote my judgment and then go home to try and persuade my constituents that I was right."

No elected representatives can satisfy all of the constituents on each issue, because the constituents are probably divided themselves.

Any representative who wins an election wins for many reasons including that a plurality or a majority of voters supported the winner. That show of support is a general endorsement of the representative's judgment.

What's a representative to do? One, present any and every idea or opinion that constituents ask to have presented at a school council meeting. Two, keep in touch with your constituents. Three, make a decision, cast a vote and move on. Decisiveness usually works better than indecisiveness. Listen, think, vote.

I'M A TEACHER, I'M NOT THE PERSON TO RUN THE SCHOOL

School-based decision making does have an impact on the job description of each teacher. By the vote for school council members, by participation in a school council committee and/or on the school council itself, teachers are now part of the school's management. The ideas, opinions and perspectives of teachers are valid because they are based upon the realities of the classroom. A huge portion of what school is happens in classrooms, so teachers can contribute to SBDM with that experience alone. No formal school administrative certification is needed.

It is important for teachers on the school council to think beyond their classroom. School council decisions need to be made for the good of the entire school, not merely for one person or for one department.

I DON'T LIKE YOU, SO I'LL VOTE AGAINST YOUR IDEA

This will occur. A parent will oppose a teacher's idea because that teacher "gave" the parent's child an "F" grade once. A teacher will oppose a parent's idea because that parent lied last month when the parent's child was not sick on Friday, but stayed home to get ready for the Saturday night prom. A principal will oppose an idea from a teacher or parent because that person called the school district's superintendent once to complain about the principal.

What is the solution? The Kentucky process for decision making is to reach decisions by consensus whenever possible. This can help get people to find common ground or to, at least, say "Well, I'm not crazy about the idea, but since most people support it, I'll go along."

It is also helpful to deal with the reality of ego, personality clashes and political battles in the training process which is provided for school council members.

I'M THE PRINCIPAL, AND I'M STILL IN CHARGE

School-based decision making does have an impact on the principal. It creates more to manage—new elections for school council members each year, preparation for each school council meeting, being the chair of or a very significant participant in school council meetings, organizing training for school council members each year and sharing the decision making authority while still being responsible for carrying out the decisions made, plus for leading the school to reach its goals.

Principals in schools with SBDM could benefit by following these aphorisms: (1) leaders do not take over, they take responsibility and (2) leadership is not doing all the jobs yourself. Leadership is working with other people to be sure that the jobs get done.

Leaders do not take over, they take responsibility.

I NEVER HEAR FROM MY CONSTITUENTS

Do they hear from you? Talk to them in person. Call them. Give them surveys or questionnaires. Knock on their doors. Send them a newsletter. Be where they go—school events, community events, the nearby grocery store and the local restaurants.

WE MAKE DECISIONS, BUT THEY DON'T GET CARRIED OUT

Make sure that people who have implementation responsibilities make progress reports at each future meeting until implementation is concluded to the group's satisfaction.

Call it follow up, follow through, execution or implementation—it is essential. Remember that the decision agenda emphasizes (1) the decision(s) to be made and (2) the assignment of duties so people know who will do what to carry out the decision. It is likely that the principal is the person who will have to hold people accountable for completion of the duties that they are assigned or that they voluntarily accept. Make sure that people who have implementation responsibilities make progress reports at each future meeting until implementation is concluded to the group's satisfaction.

THE PARENTS ONLY KNOW WHAT THEIR CHILDREN TELL THEM

Some of that student delivered information is exactly right. Some of it is inaccurate and is used by the student to cover-up his or her misbehavior or irresponsibility. Accept this fact—much of what parents/guardians know about the school or think about the school is based on what their child tells them.

There is another fact—parents/guardians know that their child is not 100% accurate or 100% honest. Do not get into battles over this; rather, give parents more information. Be sure that parents/guardians on the school council get their materials one week before the school council meetings. Try to get these parent/guardians on the school council to visit school during the day so they can see, hear and experience what their children are experiencing.

WE TALK AND TALK, BUT GET NOWHERE

There are options, such as: (1) adjourn and schedule a special meeting. (2) agree that participants do not leave until a decision is made or (3) make the decision(s) now that are possible, while delaying the decisions that cannot be made now. This last option enables groups to divide large, complex, controversial recommendations into smaller portions, some of which could be approved now while other portions need more time or study.

Limit discussion of any one item on the agenda to fifteen minutes. Keep all comments on the topic at hand. Keep all comments (a) within the areas of school council jurisdiction and (b) consistent with the school purpose. Guide all comments by use of the school's statement of purpose. Have a school council member use the parliamentary procedure process of "calling the question," which means the group is going to decide on whether members are ready to vote/reach consensus on the issue. If the group agrees to call the question, members are saying that they are ready to decide—yes or no—on the recommendation under consideration.

Follow the decision agenda. Each major topic is the school council's consideration of a recommendation from a school council committee. The group is not meeting as a school council to think out loud and start the discussion at point zero. The school council is here to agree with, disagree with or revise the recommendations that are being presented.

WE DON'T HAVE TIME FOR THESE MEETINGS

Do not have meetings monthly or on any other fixed schedule if the meeting is not needed. It is helpful to schedule the meetings for the upcoming year, but if it becomes evident in November that the November and December meetings can merge into a late November meeting, do that.

Keep the meeting on the agenda. People have time for productive, efficient meetings. People do not have time for aimless meetings.

PEOPLE DON'T LIKE THE DECISION WE MADE

Leaders are guaranteed to have opposition.

Here are two more aphorisms: (1) leaders lead and (2) leaders are guaranteed to have opposition.

School-based decision masking is not about getting everyone to like every decision. It is hoped that everyone will understand, will accept and will help implement each decision.

SBDM gives each person in the school family an opportunity to be heard, but it does not guarantee that everyone will get their way. School councils will make decisions that arouse opposition. Some decisions may be well intentioned, but after being implemented cause some unexpected and undesirable results. This gives reasons to change the decision. Mere opposition is not a reason to change a decision. Opportunities to improve a decision are reasons to make the change.

SHOULD WE LET STUDENTS ATTEND THESE MEETINGS?

The reality is that few students will be able to or will be interested enough to attend school council meetings.

The students who are chosen as voting or non-voting members of the school council may feel somewhat overwhelmed by the knowledge, age and authority of the adult members of the council.

Still, school is for students. Students need to know that they are welcome to become involved in school-based decision making or in other school improvement meetings unless confidential information will be considered.

How to Use School-Based Decision Making to Improve Specific Parts of Your School

Students, teachers, parents, and the community—if schools are to improve these groups must be committed and involved. This chapter applies decentralized management and productive meeting techniques to each of these groups. Chapter 7 concludes with a standard for everyone in the education adventure to be measured by—Results, Not Excuses.

A SUCCESSFUL SCHOOL

What are the vital variables in a successful school? Is a new set of textbooks more important than a roof that does not leak? Is a vibrant extracurricular program more helpful than a computer in each classroom? Is having each student at or above grade level in reading more important than a faculty with everyone having a master's degree? Could a school be created with all of these variables present and properly performing? If a school can have some of these, which would be selected? One good answer is "the ones which are most supportive of our school purpose."

No matter what words are used to express a school's purpose, the following ideas will probably be part of, supportive of, or consistent with school purpose:

- student learning
- teacher performance
- parent participation
- community involvement

77

- safety
- high expectations
- academic emphasis
- accountability

On the assumption that the above components could be appropriate for most school purposes, how can SBDM help in some of these areas?

SBDM AND STUDENT LEARNING

Imagine a school of 800 people. In the course of a school year each of those 800 people has one discussion about the school with each of the other 799 people. All of these discussions deal with how well students are learning or some other aspect of student learning. The total number of discussions is

$$\frac{800(799)}{2} = 319,600$$

No suggestion box could hold all of these comments if they were each written down. There is a need for a process to receive and to act upon ideas which could enhance student learning. The school council process could be used; however, similar work could be done without the legal formality of requiring SBDM. The ideas in this chapter mesh well with the formal school-based decision making process, but could be used at a school in a less formal, but equally serious process which seeks to increase participation by all concerned individually and which seeks to improve a school.

Student Learning Committee

Create a student learning committee. The committee will include students, teachers, an administrator, parents or guardians and community members. This committee will send recommendations to the school council dealing with ways to improve student learning. What's so unusual about this?

There is one uniqueness about this committee—every student is a member and every teacher is a member. How is this possible? Here's how—this committee has many subcommittees. The classes to which students report at the start of the day are all student learning subcommittees. Each classroom subcommittee has a monthly meeting to assess student learning and to create ideas that would enhance student learning. These ideas are put into recommendations which are considered at meetings of the student learning committee. This should reduce or eliminate the lament that "nobody ever asked me what I thought."

One response to this idea is, "No way. We can't involve the entire school." Now wait. The entire school will be involved in or impacted by any changes that are implemented. If a new tardy policy is established or a new dress code is implemented, each person in the school will be expected to follow the new procedure, so, of course, we can involve the whole school. The question becomes "Will the effort be made to involve everyone in discussing the problems and in creating the solutions?" The answer needs to be yes because "people support what they help create."

Yes, the adults are in charge. Yes, some very young students may suggest recess or naps as ways to improve student learning—lovely ideas, but many schools will rarely be able to implement those suggestions. If we are serious about schools having the feel of a family or of a community, we need to seriously listen to each other. School-based decision making provides the opportunity and the process for such listening.

In most schools there are three groups of people who have very reliable and very realistic perspectives on how well students are learning. The three groups are students, teachers and parents. The subcommittee system can involve each student in the process, but how can we get ideas from each teacher and parent?

Teachers need to talk (1) to each other and (2) to parents or guardians. This sounds so simple, but life gets busy, school gets busy, time gets lost and opportunities are missed. What matters most needs to be done first, so talking to each other is a high priority.

Discussion Day

Try this: one day per month is discussion day. Each teacher will use planning time or will be given planning time for an uninterrupted discussion with some colleagues about student learning. Ideas, concerns, complaints, worries, successes, failures, compliments and questions will be the order of business. There will be no personal attacks. "Thank-you" is welcome. Smiles are good. Encouragement is great. Say what needs to be said and with each comment you have to include one "next step": "OK, comments have been heard, now what can be done about those topics? Anyone can offer a next step for anyone's comment."

If it is necessary to have an assembly for students with supervision help provided by parent volunteers so time for some teachers can be created to attend the monthly discussion, do that. The "next steps" go to the school council's appropriate committee for development into recommendations or for a report on action taken by the staff to resolve the concern.

The next process is not complicated, but it is demanding. Imagine that there are 700 families in a school with sixty-two staff members. Assign twelve families to each staff member and have each staff member call his or her families once every three months. That means one phone call per week per staff member. The call is to listen and to seek ideas, not to inform. The call is to ask if there are any concerns about school, especially the level of learning by the student(s) in the family. Each call that results in a concern about school including student learning will create a note from the staff member to the principal who assigns follow-up duty to the most appropriate person. This is not complicated, but it is demanding. It could work. It could improve a school. It could identify concerns or ideas which the school council implements to benefit everyone.

SBDM AND TEACHER PERFORMANCE

Most teachers who are currently in the classroom have not been trained in school management, leadership or administration. Most teachers had college training in two broad areas: (1) how to teach and (2) the subjects they would teach.

School-based decision making says to teachers, "Welcome to the adventure of and the responsibility of leading our school." Some teachers will respond with, "It's about time that the people who know schools the best got to run the show." Others may say, "No thanks. Just leave me alone to teach. Administrators run the place."

There is a big reality that must be considered—when teachers start participating in the process of formally making decisions that impact the faculty, there is no more excuse for "us versus them" and no more rationalization of, "This would be a great school if the principal just listened to us." Now, teachers are part of the decision making process and are part of the decision implementing process. Will teacher performance in the classroom improve because teachers are part of the democratic, decentralized, participatory process of school-based decision making? Yes, if some of the decisions made by the school council are about matters which impact teacher performance.

Here's the point: SBDM will not automatically cause teacher performance in the classroom to improve. A lazy, incompetent teacher who survived under an autocratic management style will be just as lazy and incompetent under a democratic management method, unless direct action is taken.

The scientific law is that a body at rest stays at rest until acted on by an outside force. School-based decision making creates the possibility that poor or average teacher performance will remain poor or average until acted on by an *internal* force. What can SBDM do to bring about internal forces to improve poor or average teacher performance, plus to reward and encourage superior teacher performance?

Step one: listen. I once asked an outstanding teacher, "What do teachers really need from administrators?" The wise reply was, "Listen to us. Nobody just sits and listens to us with full attention and real concern. Just listen."

Another colleague told me, "Teachers need to see you do what you expect everyone to do. Don't just sit in your office. Get into the school. Take some action."

School-based decision making can be used as a method of listening and of taking action. School council committees can be the ears of the people who will make decisions for the school. There should be much listening in those meetings. School council meetings will be more opportunities for listening and for taking action.

Step two: solicit ideas. Every teacher has an idea that could improve the performance of teachers in the classroom. The ideas may range from, "Turn off the public address system," to "Give me a mental health day," to "I can't teach these special education students along with the other students. Show me what I'm supposed to do."

Whose responsibility is it to solicit ideas from teachers? Think before answering. Here's a clue—school councils are a form of representative democracy. The teacher representatives on the school council must frequently communicate with all of their colleagues. It could help if the teacher representatives divided the faculty into constituent groups so each representative kept in close touch with a portion of the faculty. Some schools will prefer to avoid that subdivision process and have all teacher representatives on the school council keep in touch with all teachers.

Please note, teachers need to make the effort to contact their school council representatives. Don't let faculty lounge gossip or after hours griping pass for real contribution to discussion of ways to improve the school. Eliminate the gossip. Challenge teachers to match each criticism of the school they utter with a suggestion that addresses the problem. Talk to a school council member about concerns and suggestions. Attend a committee meeting and help write the recommendation. Ask other teachers for their ideas and for their support. Attend the school council meeting and lobby for concerns to be addressed and for recommendations to be approved, even if amended.

Step three: emphasize the classroom. When ideas that impact teacher performance are brought to the school council, each idea has to pass the classroom test: How will this idea help students and teachers in the classroom? The high priority work in school happens in the classrooms. Much school council time and effort should be directed to this high priority. Other topics will merit attention and effort, but in proportion to their importance rather than in proportion to any other factor.

No matter what words a school has in its statement of school purpose, it is likely that the emphasis is on student learning. To the extent that a school council devotes time to topics that relate to and ideas that improve what happens in the classroom, that school council will move closer to fulfilling any school purpose that emphasizes student learning.

Step four: teacher interaction. Create a school council committee which reports progress made in classrooms on any topic the other school council committees are considering. Here's the idea: every problem at a school has already been solved at another school which had the same or a similar problem. Here's the hope—every problem at a school is already being addressed by at least one teacher at that school. How many teachers know what all of their colleagues at their school are doing to reach goals and solve problems? Right—very few, so teacher interaction needs to increase.

This sequence could work—the school council agrees to assign a revision of the homework policy to the curriculum committee. Before that committee meets, the communication committee will obtain input from each teacher. What homework procedure gets the best results in your classroom? What method gets the highest rate of homework being turned in? How often do you give homework—why is that the right schedule?

The results of this survey and/or of face-to-face discussions becomes the basis of the curriculum committee's work.

Why not have the curriculum committee do their own surveys? Some people are great at improving the curriculum. Some people are great at getting teacher input on any subject. SBDM is improved as each person applies his or her unique abilities.

Step five: _____

_____

_____

_____

_____

What was written? What way was created for school-based decision making to help improve teacher performance. Step five could get the most results because the author of step five knows what will work best at his or her school.

Warning—some people will oppose any change. Some people will oppose every change. Schools are in their present condition for many reasons including these facts—some people are satisfied, some people are lazy, some people are not smart, some people are coasting until retirement and some schools are doing a good job.

The goal is to improve schools. The goal is not to make everyone happy. It is important to seek consensus, but school improvement cannot wait forever as people seek to reach consensus. SBDM taps new sources of ideas and involvement, but it does not change human nature. School-based decision making does not replace good leadership, it builds upon and complements good leadership. In fact, SBDM asks more people to become leaders in each school.

SBDM AND PARENT PARTICIPATION IN SCHOOL

Time. One of the most relentless problems any school council will face as it tries to increase parent participation is the high number of demands on the schedules of parents and guardians. How many of these people have the time and the flexibility in their schedules to attend school council meetings, to attend committee meetings, to read enough to fully understand school issues and to visit school often enough to feel part of it?

"The school can't do it all. We need help from parents." One of the most common comments heard in any school is that parental participation is essential. Can SBDM be the process which bridges the gap between limited parental time and unlimited need for parental involvement?

The answer is a very honest—"maybe." Schools have some parental participation now. When a school begins using school-based decision making it is possible that the parents who are already involved will be the only parents who participate on the school council. What can be done?

Step one: tell every parent and guardian what a school council is. School councils did not exist when those parents or guardians went to school or when their younger children went to school. Each family needs to be told what a school council is. Take the approach that a company takes when introducing a new product—advertise, set up displays, have promotions or contests, and give free samples. How? Here are some possible actions to take:

(1) Advertise
   • Get radio and television stations to run free "public service ads" about school councils.
   • Have local companies and civic groups adopt the school council so they can tell their employees, customers, members or service recipients.
   • Send news releases about the school council to the local media.
   • Now think of more ways to advertise to parents and guardians:
   •

   •

   •

   •

(2) Displays
   • Have students create posters about SBDM and place these in grocery stores, churches, recreation facilities, any place the adults of the school community go.
   • Have a booth at any county fair, church festival or sports event including school sports activities.

- Create a brochure about SBDM and put copies of it on the counter of each business that will cooperate.
- Give a copy of the brochure for each student to take home.
- Create more display ideas . . .
-
-
-
-

(3) Promotions
- Have a school council meeting that is also a picnic or pot luck supper.
- Combine a school council meeting at 6:00 P.M. with a student presentation—theater, band, orchestra, chorus, athletics—at 7:30 P.M.
- Have a school council meeting as a "Parents Night Out" on Friday. The school council meets from 6:00–7:30 after a pizza supper at 5:30. At 7:30 show a movie. At the same time free baby-sitting is provided in the gym with help from teachers and high school students.
- More ideas, please:
-
-
-

(4) Free samples
- With help from a media expert in your school, a local television station or at the nearest university, create a video about SBDM and distribute this to parents who pass it on to other parents according to the list of neighbors placed on the container of each copy of the video.

- Get the local cable television company to broadcast your school council meeting. Imagine—the SBDM channel!
- Make an audio tape about school-based decision making. Use voices of local radio or television celebrities and/or of local community leaders. Distribute this to parents as you did the video.
- More ideas, please:
-
-
-
-

The simple process of making a phone call to each parent is still needed even if some of the marketing ideas listed above are used. Divide the school families among all parents who will make monthly phone calls. Maybe each person will have ten to twenty families to call each month. The call is to give information and to get information. The callers meet monthly to summarize what they have heard so the school council gets that information.

> The school council needs to show parents that what already concerns them and perplexes them about their children are some of the issues that the school council is dealing with. Families and schools need each other. School councils can be the process through which that mutual need is put into mutually beneficial action.

Time demands on parents and guardians will not become less and may become more. SBDM will not get involvement from uninvolved parents if the school council appears as one more demand on time, energy and other limited resources. The school council needs to show parents that what already concerns them and perplexes them about their children are some of the issues that the school council is dealing with. Families and schools need each other. School councils can be the process through which that mutual need is put into mutually beneficial action.

For parents who have always sought ways to be involved in schools, SBDM is a superior opportunity. For parents who say "I just can't find out what is going on at the school," SBDM gives them a voice and a vote about what is going on, plus it makes information available that can help explain why schools function as they do. For parents who are angry about schools, SBDM can replace the nasty letters that used to be sent or the ugly phone calls that used to be made. SBDM can enable people to change that anger into productive action—if those people really intended to be productive and not just sound off.

For parents who have said, "The school just does not listen to me," now the school has a new listening system—the school council and the many committees serving the council. For parents and guardians who are willing to team up with schools, school-based decision making is the process that changes the "us versus them" battles that parents and schools sometimes endure, into "us with us" so everyone associated with and concerned about the school works together.

If parents will make the time to attend school council meetings, if parents will make the effort to attend committee meetings, if parents will read books and articles about education issues, if parents will bring their knowledge about children, then parents can be a potent force for improving schools via school-based decision making.

Schools must make these requests for parents and guardians—please do not use SBDM as a way to get anything extra for your child, please do not use SBDM to express your criticism of individuals, please do not use SBDM as the arena where your neighborhood arguments are expanded and please do not preface your comments, with "My child told me. . . ." Think of all students, all teachers, all parents and the total school. Help improve the school for everyone. SBDM is not a process for the personal agenda, ego or emotions of one person to be expressed. SBDM is of, by, and for everyone.

SBDM AND COMMUNITY INVOLVEMENT

It is often stated that 30% of adult Americans have children who attend a public school. The other 70% of adult Americans have no children, have children who are younger than or older than the ages during which school is attended or have enrolled their children in private schools.

This same 70% of adult Americans pay taxes for public schools, employ graduates of public schools, live next door to students who attend public schools and have nephews, nieces, or grandchildren in public schools. The schools and the community share this adventure and this duty of education or society suffers.

I do not like to attend events that attract huge crowds; however, such events do get my attention. Sports, concerts or political demonstrations intellectually intrigue me, but I prefer not to be in the big crowd. I do appreciate being asked to go to such events. It means something to me that another person would want me to be at the big event with them. My common response to such an invitation is, "I'm honored that you would ask me. I'm not much for big crowds, but I'd love to see you. Let's have supper together next week—my treat. You can tell me about the event. What night is best for you?"

That story relates to using SBDM as a way to increase community involvement in schools. First, people appreciate being asked. Second, if people reject the initial offer, another plan can be made.

Can school officials identify each resident of the area that sends students to the school? Yes. If they can be identified, they can be contacted. How? Phone calls, letters, brochures distributed door-to-door are options. There is probably a parent or guardian on each block of each street, or at least on each street, in most schools' attendance districts. Using block leaders, or street leaders, you could easily get information about the school to community members and you could get ideas, input, criticism and concern from those same community members.

How could the school-based decision making process and structure be used to increase community involvement? List ten ideas below, please. It's OK to adapt ideas that were mentioned earlier.

(1)

(2)

(3)

(4)

(5)

(6)

(7)

(8)

(9)

(10)

School-based decision making is a political process. School council members get elected. Some tax money may be allocated by the school council if the council has budget authority. Constituents need to be heard. A school council that reaches out to the community is wise and conscientious in its professional, ethical and political duties.

SBDM—THE BUCK STOPS WITH ME

Put simply, the challenge now is "Results, Not Excuses."

The success of the practical process of school-based decision making depends upon teachers, administrators, students, parents, guardians and the community taking responsibility for their school. The blame game is over. There are no excuses. SBDM gives authority and responsibility for each school to the people who have always said, "Nobody ever asked me," or "I could show them how to run a school." Put simply, the challenge now is, "Results, Not Excuses."

For anyone who ever said, "Nobody ever asked me." OK, schools are asking now. Come to the school council meetings. Serve on the council or on a school council committee. Help improve the school. The motive is to improve schools. The opportunity of school-based decision making, of similar school-based improvement processes or of school-based management can help schools, families and communities do what always should have been done—work together to improve schools.

Ready, Set, Go: A Checklist for Introducing SBDM

School-based decision making happens in one school at a time, in one school council meeting at a time. Long before that first school council meeting can occur, some serious thought must be applied by state and/or local education leaders to the process by which SBDM will be started. This appendix helps explain that process.

As the idea of and the use of school-based decision making becomes common, each school which creates a school council can apply the pioneering SBDM work from Chicago, Kentucky and other places where SBDM has been a vital part of school reform in the late 1980s and in the 1990s.

Kentucky's education reform law is known as KERA—The Kentucky Education Reform Act. This law was passed in April 1990. KERA required each of Kentucky's 176 school districts to establish a policy about SBDM by January 1, 1991. Each school district had to have at least one school using school-based decision making during the 1991–1992 school year. With limited exceptions, all Kentucky public schools are required to have SBDM by 1996–1997. As of 1996, two-thirds of the public schools in Kentucky, by a vote of the teachers in each participating school, had already begun using school-based decision making.

The reasons for Kentucky schools to begin SBDM ahead of schedule include the reality that the 1996 implementation requirement is inevitable, so why wait; however, the stronger reasons come in the success stories from schools that have significantly improved in many ways due to the process of school-based decision making.

Before those SBDM success stories could occur, a process for beginning and implementing school-based decision making was needed. In Kentucky, the school districts primarily followed guidelines from the Kentucky Department of Education and a model SBDM policy developed by the Kentucky School Boards Association in creating their policies on school-based decision making. There were at least thirteen topics which almost all school districts included in their SBDM policies. Where mandates were established in the Kentucky Education Reform Act, no variance in policies existed across the many school districts. Where KERA did not specify the content of SBDM policy, school districts made their own decisions.

The following summary includes the thirteen topics which Kentucky school districts included in their SBDM polices and some precedents from Kentucky. The summary also includes some details of the more specific actions which must be taken in order to implement school-based decision making and the areas in which decisions should be made before SBDM can begin at a school. The summary is not limited to practices from Kentucky, but is based on the Kentucky experience with SBDM.

1. *The request to consider having a school council:* This could be done by requiring that a certain percentage of teachers must sign a petition, which then leads to the entire faculty voting on whether to have a school council or not. Some school boards or state legislatures may mandate school-based decision making thus making this step unnecessary. In the absence of such mandates in law or in school board policy, a petition from the faculty is a reasonable way to gauge the interest in a formal vote to have SBDM.

Please note that since school-based decision making involves teachers, administrators, students, parents, guardians, and community members, it may be important to have several options which lead to the decision to begin SBDM. If the parents of a school supported the idea of school-based decision making, but the teachers opposed the idea, it may be desirable to have a method to prevent one group from blocking the initial consideration of having SBDM.

2. *Voting to begin SBDM:* Step 1 was for the faculty and/or another group to request a vote on the school entering into SBDM. After that request has been properly made, who will vote on having SBDM? Teachers only? What percentage of teachers must approve? All school employees? Parents and guardians? Should each group which would be involved in the school council be involved in this vote to enter SBDM?

In Kentucky, when 25% of the teachers in a school petitioned to have a vote on SBDM, the vote was held. KERA required a two-thirds vote of the faculty to formally authorize the start of school-based decision making at any school. Initially, many school districts placed limits on how often a faculty could vote to enter SBDM, but some of those limits were relaxed or removed over time.

3. *Repeal of SBDM:* Kentucky schools were given the option to consider repealing school-based decision making (a) if they began SBDM prior to 1996 and (b) knowing that in 1996 they would have to begin using SBDM again, with few exceptions. The repeal process probably has little merit because schools have found that having SBDM is beneficial and the 1996 mandate is inevitable.

4. *Models:* KERA established school council membership to be three teachers, two parents, and one administrator. A school could increase the size if the same 3:2:1 proportion was kept. Schools could request that alternative models be approved, but the Kentucky Department of Education was reluctant to approve alternatives.

Other states or school districts have included classified employees, community members, and/or students on school councils.

5. *Electing school council members:* Step one is the determination of school council membership. The principal needs to be a member automatically, but beyond that the best combination of teachers, staff members, parents/guardians, students, and community members will vary based on the needs of a state, school district or school. It is reasonable that each of the constituent groups would elect their own representative(s) to the school council.

Kentucky requires that each teacher who is elected to the school council must have a majority of the votes of the faculty. If you are electing six teacher members to the school council and ten teachers nominated themselves or accepted nominations, each faculty member could cast six votes initially. The first ballot may create majorities for six teachers, but subsequent ballots may be needed if fewer than six teachers received a majority vote on the first ballot. It may be useful to require the same majority vote of all parents participating in the voting. Kentucky's school councils do not include classified staff members, students or community members as voting participants; however, serious consideration for including these groups as voting or as non-voting members is encouraged.

6. *School council authority:* This is a matter for legislatures, school boards, school councils and courts to resolve. What can a state govern-

ment mandate, what can a school board require and how much real freedom does a school council have to make decisions for a school given the realities of state laws and local school board policies?

The Kentucky Education Reform Act assigned eight areas of authority to school councils [KRS Chapter 160, section 14 (2) (I) (7-18)].

(1) Determination of curriculum, including needs assessment, curriculum development, alignment with state standards, technology utilization, and program appraisal within the local school board's policy
(2) Assignment of all instructional and non-instructional staff time
(3) Assignment of students to classes and programs within the school
(4) Determination of the schedule of the school day and week, subject to the beginning and ending times of the school day and school calendar as established by the local board
(5) Determination of use of school space during the school day
(6) Planning and resolution of issues regarding instructional practices
(7) Selection and implementation of discipline and classroom management techniques, including responsibilities of the student, parent, teacher, counselor, and principal
(8) Selection of extracurricular programs and determination of policies relating to student participation based on academic qualifications and attendance requirements, program evaluation and supervision.

It should be noted that the Kentucky Supreme Court upheld the authority of school councils in a December 1994 decision. Some school boards and the Kentucky School Boards Association were concerned that school councils were taking too much authority from school boards. The court concluded in its review of *Board of Education of Boone County, Kentucky v. Joan Bushee et al.*

Each participating group in the common school system has been delegated its own independent sphere of responsibility. State government is held accountable for providing adequate funding and for the overall success of the common school system. The local boards are responsible for the administrative functions of allocating funding, managing school property, appointing the superintendent, and fixing the compensation of employees. The councils are responsible for the site based issues, including but not limited to, determining curriculum, planning instructional priorities, selecting and implementing discipline techniques, determining the composition of the staff at the school, and choosing textbooks and instructional materials.

7. *School council meetings:* How many school council members must be present to have a quorum? How will decisions be made—consensus, vote? If a vote is taken, is a simple majority or a greater majority required for approval of action? How often will meetings be held? Where and at what time of day will meetings be held? Should meetings always be at the school?

Kentucky law requires that school council meetings are open to the public. This is a good place to emphasize that school council meetings are not to become personnel or personal discussions of teachers, students, parents, or other people. When such matters need attention, the school administrators should take appropriate action in a legal, humane, and professional way. School councils are for ideas, policies, and decisions.

It is not productive to discuss topics at school council meetings over which the school council has no jurisdiction. The council could ask its chairperson to communicate with the person or group with authority on such topics.

It is not professional or ethical to discuss individuals at school council meetings. Such personal and personnel matters are to be managed by administrators.

It is wrong for school councils to knowingly violate law or school board policy. School councils have plenty to do that is legal. There is no need to explore or to usurp other tasks. Of course, school councils may seek waivers from school board policies and school councils may challenge laws; however, pre-emptive actions which are inconsistent with policy or law would be counterproductive.

8. *School council relationships:* Most people associated with schools today have not been involved with school councils. An energetic effort will be needed to teach people associated with a school about the process of school-based decision making.

9. *School council polices, including waivers:* The importance of committees and recommendations in the SBDM process is well established. The school council will need to decide whether a policy can be adopted at the first meeting in which it is presented or if it is better to allow time to

pass so more people hear of the proposed policy and then action could be taken at the next meeting. A waiver option of such a two meeting provision will enable the school council to act immediately as needed.

In matters over which school councils do not have total jurisdiction, Kentucky school councils occasionally pass policies that are different from the policy of the local school board for the entire school district. For example, a school council may approve a policy that changes grades "F" and "D" to "not finished yet." The student must improve his or her work until it reaches the "C" level. The local school board would be asked to approve a waiver from the school district's established grading scale *prior* to the new policy going into practice. This is a reasonable way to resolve matters in which (a) a school council and the school board have shared interests and perhaps, shared jurisdiction or (b) the school board has jurisdiction but can provide flexibility to meet needs of individual schools.

10. *Appeal of decisions:* SBDM increases the likelihood of broad input to and support for decisions that will improve schools; however, people who oppose an action of the school council deserve an appeals process. This process could have several steps that include all or some of the following: the school council committee that studied the topic, the school council, the local school district's superintendent, and the local school board. Please note: on matters over which the school council has jurisdiction, the superintendent or the school board could not reverse a school council's action unless a procedural error could be proven. If the school council violated its own by-laws, school board policies, or state law, the appeal to the superintendent or to the school board would be more likely to have merit.

11. *School budget and purchasing:* Education remains a duty of state governments acting through local school boards. The financing of public education is not a duty assigned to school councils; however, the school council should have the authority to allocate funds that are budgeted to or assigned to a school. These funds could cover textbooks, office supplies, instructional materials, professional travel, and other monies that relate directly to the areas over which the school council has authority. School councils should follow local school board policies and applicable state laws in all purchases. This includes using sensible accounting, bookkeeping, and bidding procedures so expenditures are properly managed to give taxpayers the best return on their investment in education.

12. *School hiring:* School-based decision making can involve the en-

tire school council or a committee in the personnel process. This may not be required. Some school districts may have processes that involve only the superintendent in the hiring process or the superintendent and the principal of the school that has a vacancy may decide together.

The Kentucky process requires the principal to "consult" with the school council before any vacancy is filled. It is becoming common for a principal to include some school council members in the interviews with candidates for a job at the school. The principal consults with the school council members after the interviews are completed to see if there is consensus. The principal reserves the right to make the final decision unless he or she chooses to defer to the others involved in the consultation. When there is a vacancy in the job of principal, the full school council interviews candidates who have been screened by the local school district's personnel staff and whose names have been provided by the superintendent.

13. *Training of school council members:* Teachers have been taught about teaching, not about leading or managing schools; however, teachers have insight into the many factors that impact a school or into conditions at a school. Parents, guardians, staff members, students, and community members have not studied or been responsible for school management or leadership; however, they have ideas, concerns, questions, and judgment.

To successfully implement SBDM, each school will need to train the school council members in topics that range from representing constituents to managing school budgets.

Questions and Answers

Assume that a state and/or school district has approved a law and/or school board policy that explains how school-based decision making can, if optional, or must, if mandated, be implemented. It is also possible that in the absence of such a law or policy a school could just voluntarily decide to form a school council so decision making becomes a shared process. That is fine, but realize that in the case of such a voluntary action, the authority given to such a school council will be limited to (a) what the person or people currently in charge will share and (b) the authority which state law and school board policies give to individual schools. The fact is this—the school is going to begin using school-based decision making.

What needs to be done to get SBDM started? A report needs to be written. This report will be presented at three meetings: (1) a faculty meeting, (2) a parent and community member meeting and (3) an assembly of the student body. Here's the outline of the report with extra space for more ideas to be written in:

OUTLINE

(1) SBDM—What it is
  • decentralized management
  • participatory
  • democratic
  • limited to specific jurisdiction

- an increase in responsibility an individual school has for its performance
- an increase in the school's accountability for each student
-
-
-

(2) SBDM—Why we are starting it
- A new law requires it.
- Our school board is requiring it.
- It is our voluntary decision.
- Other schools have had good results with this.
- Our people know our school best.
-
-
-

(3) SBDM—How we will get started
- several informational meetings such as this
- written materials given to students, families, teachers, staff, and the community
- a vote of teachers and parents/guardians
- if approved, a school task force to write our proposed SBDM by-laws
-
-
-

(4) What you can do now
- Read all materials about SBDM that are distributed.
- Attend the informational meetings.

-

-

-

(5) Questions
  - These would not all be answered immediately—some would need a letter, phone call or conversation in person after the answer is found.
  - Have a person experienced in SBDM attend the meeting so as many answers as possible can be given.
  -

  -

  -

QUESTIONS AND ANSWERS

Some questions that would be asked can be anticipated. Some answers are listed and some room is provided for answers to be written.

(1) How do we keep people from using the school council for their personal agenda?
  - Establish a clear school purpose and keep school council discussions within the purpose.
  - Provide training for school council members so they understand their duty.
  -

  -

(2) How will my opinion get expressed if I'm not a member of the school council?
  - Meetings will be open to the public and may include time for comments from the audience.

- Have one or more council members represent your ideas.
- Become a member of a school council committee.
- Submit your ideas to the council in writing.
-
-

(3) This sounds like a lot of work. Who has time for all of these meetings?
- If you really do not have the time, do not seek a position on the school council.
- If you absolutely cannot attend a meeting, you can notify the chair in advance—the by-laws should have a provision about attendance requirements.
-
-

(4) What happens if people resign from the school council before their term ends?
- A special election is held to fill the vacancy for the remainder of the term.
- The by-laws could give the school council the authority to appoint a temporary member.
- The council can still have a quorum if a member resigns.
-
-

(5) Do we have to do this?
- In Kentucky the answer is yes, the law requires this.
- If SBDM is optional, the answer could be "We get to do this. The research shows that this can work."
-
-

(6) Can you get kicked off the school council?
  - The by-laws may include a section with a process for removing council members due to poor attendance or other specific reasons.
  -
  -

(7) You know how teachers complain about school all the time in the faculty lounge. Will they really start using the school council process or will they just keep complaining in the lounge?
  - Some will keep complaining, but let's not allow them to prevent this from helping our school.
  - Teachers need to discipline themselves and their colleagues so faculty lounge discussion is proper.
  -
  -

(8) What if we get tired of this in a few years or what if the old way was better?
  - If SBDM is required, for now, we have to accept the law or the policy that requires this, but we could try to get the law or policy changed.
  - If SBDM is optional, we could decide to end SBDM just as we decided to start it.
  -
  -

(9) What about parents who get on the school council and just look after their own children?
  - Their constituents need to vote them off the school council in the next election.
  - The council chair will direct discussion to the school's statement of purpose and away from personal politics.
  -

•

(10) Why does every teacher have to be on a committee?
   • Every teacher has ideas to offer. The committee system efficiently processes those ideas.
   • For SBDM to work best, all teachers should participate.
   • It is part of the new job description of a teacher.
   •

   •

(11) What if not enough people run for the school council?
   • We would still have an election to see if the candidates get supported or not. Any vacant seats would be filled according to the by-laws.
   • This may suggest that the size of the council is too large.
   •

   •

(12) What happens if members can't come to a meeting and no action can be taken?
   • That happens in any representative body. The council could schedule a special meeting or just wait for the next regular meeting.
   • The by-laws may need an emergency provision that allows temporary action to be taken in the absence of a quorum. The action must be confirmed at the next school council meeting or it is nullified.
   •

   •

(13) Do you think the school council will try to run everything in the school?

- The school council will have specific jurisdiction with limits.

- The council cannot control the areas which are reserved to the state government or to the local school board.

-

-

(14) Won't some people still complain that nobody asked them for their opinion even after the school council invites people to participate.
   - Yes and that may never change.
   - Yes and those people need to be encouraged to participate in the school council or be asked to be quiet while other people lead the way.

   -

   -

(15) Do you get paid extra for being on the school council?
   - No. This duty is part of being an educator, parent/guardian or citizen.
   - Not in cash, but we reap rewards in the results we get for our school.

   -

   -

(16) How are school council decisions implemented? Who follows up?
   - Each school council meeting can include a progress report on past decisions. This continues until a decision is fully implemented.
   - When the school council makes a decision it simultaneously assigns implementation duty to specific people.

   -

   -

There will be many other questions. There will be some trials and errors. There will be some growing pains.

There will be many answers and ideas, recommendations and proposals, problems solved and problems evaded. There will be obstacles overcome and new results obtained. There will be some victories.

School-based decision making has already proven its worth as a management and leadership process for building consensus for decisions which improve schools. Through vibrant, effective management of school council meetings—including all necessary preparation for those meetings and all proper follow-up after those meetings—schools can be improved.

Our goal is to improve each school. School-based decision making is one solid way of reaching that goal. Having productive meetings of school councils will help make SBDM work at your school.

Dr. Keen J. Babbage has taught grades 7–12, college, and graduate school. He has executive experience with three large corporations, and he has school administration experience with grades 6–12.

Dr. Babbage has earned degrees from Centre College, Xavier University, and the University of Kentucky. His doctoral work at Kentucky was during 1989–1993 as the Kentucky Education Reform Act was developed, approved, and initially implemented.

Dr. Babbage's dissertation dealt with the public policy process of implementing school-based decision making.

He lives and works in Lexington, Kentucky.